Also by Richard Barber

The Figure of Arthur

King Arthur

Henry Plantagenet

The Knight and Chivalry

Samuel Pepys Esq

A Dictionary of Fabulous Beasts
(with Anne Riches)

RICHARD BARBER

Cooking and Recipes from Rome to the Renaissance

ALLEN LANE

First published in 1973

Allen Lane
A Division of Penguin Books Ltd
21 John Street, London W C I

IS B N 0 7139 0489 5

Printed in Great Britain
by W & J Mackay Limited, Chatham

Contents

List of Plates

List of Line Illustrations

The decoration above each recipe section is a sixteenth-century wood-cut of a French kitchen.

Introduction

The art of cookery is much older than the oldest recipes we possess; but without the recipes we can only describe the methods of cookery, not the means and ingredients. A history of cookery could well begin with the inventor in the Old Stone Age who discovered that roasted food had a better flavour and kept longer than raw meat. About the same time men also discovered that if you dropped a hot stone into a mixture of herbs and water the flavour of the herbs was quickly transferred to the heated water. Neither of these methods required elaborate tools: a couple of sticks held meat over the fire and natural rock pools provided the containers for primitive soups. Old Stone Age men won their food by hunting or by gathering wild plants, and these simple techniques were enough to deal with their limited range of diet. New Stone Age men, however, had a different system of food-gathering, and so needed new ways of dealing with their raw materials. From gathering and hunting, they had changed to planting and breeding; instead of being hunters, they were farmers. Grain was easy enough to grow, but could be eaten only if made into a moist mixture which would serve either as porridge or as a crude dough for flat cakes cooked on stones heated in an open fire. Oatmeal cakes are perhaps the nearest to a survival from prehistoric cookery that can still be found today.

Until the late New Stone Age period, which corresponds roughly with the beginnings of the earliest civilizations in the Middle East, the storage and preparation of raw food were still much more important than cookery. The 'cook' was not a cook in our sense of the word, but a storekeeper. With the introduction of much more elaborate machinery for farming, particularly the plough, there also came a revolution in the cook's methods. Better pottery was available, which could be used to boil liquids over the fire, and these vessels were made in metal in the Iron and Bronze Ages which followed. Cooking in an enclosed dry container heated from outside – the principle of baking – was another discovery of the period, and stewing and frying appeared soon afterwards. All these changes were an integral part of the new style of life in the towns and villages of the Middle and Near East.

In the earliest written records of Egypt and Sumeria (modern Iraq), there is much information about what was eaten, and Egyptian tomb paintings depict many different cooking processes; but the vital details of how the individual ingredients were put together has not survived. The idea of combining different flavours, which is the essence of cookery as opposed to cooking, was certainly still in its infancy. We do learn that onions, leeks and garlic were used with other vegetables, and that cakes were bound together with honey or oil before frying or baking. The earliest sweets, also based on honey, were invented, and the range of foods was very wide. Only pork and root vegetables were absent from Egyptian diet, and pork was common in Sumeria. The pestle and mortar were used for herbs, and wheat was ground into flour using millstones turned by hand. Milling and baking were much more efficient if carried out with special equipment, and millers and bakers appeared as specialist tradesmen at a very early date. Even if Egyptian cookery was very much simpler than that of ancient Greece and Rome, the beginnings were nonetheless there. Spices such as sesame, caraway and poppyseed were used on bread, and there is a mention of a kind of sharp sauce made from vinegar or sour grape juice to accompany fish. Two basic items which were first widely used in Egypt (we take them so much for granted today that it is hard to imagine them being invented) were bread made with yeast, and wine. The effect of yeast on bread was not properly understood by the Egyptians who always kept part of the previous day's dough to activate the new dough instead of adding the yeast alone. Although the techniques of wine-making may have been discovered before the period of the earliest written records, wine always remained a luxury in Sumeria, where most of the inhabitants drank beer. The names of popular brands of beer have come down to us, and brewing was an organized industry rather than a household activity. Wine is recorded only in royal documents from Sumeria, while in Egypt it was an everyday drink. A Greek legend tells how Dionysos, the god of wine, fled from Sumeria to Egypt because the Sumerians were addicted to beer, and later came to Greece from Egypt.

The development of cookery runs parallel with two other developments in ancient civilization: the growth of cities and the creation of long-distance trade-routes. People living in cities made no attempt to live off their own produce, and were therefore free to choose between different kinds of food, while the farmers were limited in their choice to the foods which grew best on their own land, or which they could obtain in exchange for their own goods. As demand for different kinds of foods and for greater choice developed, it became worthwhile to organize trading expeditions, and both ancient Egypt and Greece drew on a wide area for their goods. Traders went as far as India in search of spices and precious materials such as gold, jewels, ivory and minerals, and as they cast their net ever wider, so the variety of foodstuffs and the ways in which they were prepared was extended. This was a gradual process, and it is only in fifth-century Greece that our story really begins. Only then did the cook have a sufficient range of resources at his disposal to create an art of his own.

In what follows, I have tried to map out the main lines of European cookery from classical Greece down to the end of the seventeenth century. The source material is fairly limited, as there are few surviving cookery books, and little work has yet been done to establish the 'family tree' that links them. In two areas I have had to admit defeat: I have not been able to explore the history of Spanish cookery, important though it is, because so much of it is Arabic in origin and requires a much more detailed investigation of Arabic cookery than I have been able to carry out; nor is the account of German cookery more than a footnote, because the only copies in Britain of many of the books were destroyed during the last war. So this book is only a first sketch of a very fascinating subject, perhaps it will encourage others to fill in the details.

The end of the seventeenth century may seem a rather unusual place to end. However, eighteenth-century cookery is not so very different from that of today. Early in the eighteenth century, cookery becomes much more national, and English cooks in particular turn away from Continental cookery to domestic cookery instead. The instructions in cookery books become much clearer as they are written more and more for the home rather than for a nobleman's kitchen. Recipes from books like Hannah Glasse's in the mid-eighteenth century need no special translation for a modern cook, since materials, methods and implements are all very similar to those of today.

I   Greece and Rome:
Cookery as the New Art

Figure 1 A provincial Roman dinner party as imagined by a sixteenth-century artist.

Greek cooking begins very simply. The heroes of Homer live off a farmer's diet of oxen, pigs and sheep, and their banquets are not adorned by elaborate rarities. Even the scale of their feasts seems modest, and the highest compliment a guest can receive is to be given the chine of an ox. Fish and fowl are absent from their tables, and it is only when Odysseus and his comrades are near starvation on the island of Thrinacia that they set out 'with barbed hooks in search of game, fishes or anything that might come to hand'. Fruit and vegetables appear only occasionally: pears, figs, pomegranates and apples. Onions were used as a kind of appetizer served with spiced wine. Cheese was another staple food.

All this reflects a way of life in which the tending of flocks was the source of even a king's revenue. And the heroes themselves did not hesitate to lend a hand in the preparations. Here is the scene at Achilles' tent, when Odysseus arrives to appease Achilles and heal the quarrel between him and Agamemnon:

Patroclus carried out his comrade's orders. He put down a big bench in the firelight, and laid on it the backs of a sheep and a fat goat and the chine of a great hog rich in lard. Automedon held these for him, while Achilles jointed them, and then carved up the joints and spitted the slices. Meanwhile, Patroclus, the royal son of Menoetius, made the fire blaze up. When it had burnt down again and the flames had disappeared, he scattered the embers and laid the spits above them, resting them on dogs, after he had sprinkled the meat with holy salt. When he had roasted it and heaped it up on platters, Patroclus fetched some bread and set it out on the table in handsome baskets; and Achilles divided the meat into portions.

It is a far cry from this noble simplicity to the luxuries of fourth-century Athens. The city was defeated in the Peloponnesian Wars by Sparta, and it was in the unheroic days of Spartan domination that cookery as an art began to flourish in Greece. Perhaps it was a reaction to the favourite diet of the conquerors. There was a story that a man from Sybaris, the Greek colony in southern Italy renowned for its luxury, had once been to Sparta, where he attended a public dinner. (The Spartans fed communally, rather like the inhabitants of Sir Thomas More's Utopia.) The main dish was the notorious Spartan black broth, compounded of the lights of pork and a fierce seasoning. The astonished Sybarite remarked afterwards: 'It is no wonder that Spartans are the bravest men in the world; for anyone in his right mind would prefer to die ten thousand times rather than share in such poor living.'

So it was to Sybaris and Sicily that the Athenians turned in their quest for distraction. We are accustomed to thinking of southern Italy and Sicily as backward, poverty-stricken regions but only centuries of misrule have made them so. Once these lands were among the richest in the Mediterranean, eagerly sought by land-hungry Greek colonists; and it had been Athens's eagerness to conquer these prizes that had led to her downfall. Instead, Sicily conquered Athens – in the kitchen. As far as we can tell, it was Sicilian and Sybarite cooks who first explored the imaginative possibilities of cookery. Other nations may have sought out rare and exotic ingredients, as the Persians certainly did, but it was here that invention was first appreciated. In Sybaris 'if any caterer or cook invented a dish which was especially choice' no one save the inventor was allowed to adopt the use of it before a year had passed, a kind of primitive copyright in food. It is this passion for novelty which marks – and often mars – both Greek and Roman cookery in the succeeding centuries. Cookery was to become 'no mere trade, but a natural gift, a special art, a school of philosophy'.

Only fragments survive of the works of these pioneering Sicilian cooks, who either by travelling to Athens or by sending copies of their recipes laid the foundations for a new concept of eating. Even so, it took time for their ideas to be widely adopted. In the third century B.C., Athenian dinners were still served, as the satirists pointed out, 'all-at-once, in the grand style', meaning that it was the impression of quantity and variety that mattered, not the skill with which the dishes had been prepared. As tastes grew more fastidious, the meal was divided into courses. At first, dishes of meat and fish would form the main course, followed by shell-fish and vegetables; later the order was reversed. Then these widely varying courses were separated and elaborated, so that a Greek epicure's dinner eventually had four main divisions. An *hors d'œuvre*, not so far removed from our modern version in its ingredients, was followed by roast or boiled fish and meat, stews and vegetables; the next course was made up of the main dishes, the chef's special creations, and of fried dishes; and the meal ended with dessert.

Manners and methods of serving also became more important as food grew from a necessity into a luxury. Originally the guests would have been seated, and this custom survived for another five centuries among the simpler or more conservative families. The gourmets, however, 'began to luxuriate and have degenerate manners': 'They slid from chairs to couches, and taking as their ally relaxation and ease, from this time on they indulged in the carouse in lax and disorderly fashion, being seduced into pleasure, I fancy, by their rich surroundings.'

The author from whom this rather puritan remark comes is a certain Athenaeus, whose immense treatise on Greek dining and food was written in the third century A.D. It is he who has preserved for us most of our information about early Greek cookery and its history, buried among the twenty books of *The Deipnosophists*, a title which can be roughly translated as *The Wise Men at Dinner*. The work is presented as a dialogue between the guests at an imaginary feast, and the conversation is largely about food and dinner parties. His guests, indeed, are so learned, and produce such a flood of words on subjects ranging from drinking cups, gluttony, music and Plato the philosopher, by way of wreaths, after-dinner games and lamps, to literary parodies and famous prostitutes, that food does become something of an after-thought. But because he is the only Greek writer on cookery whose work has survived reasonably intact we have to forgive him his endless digressions, his tantalizing vagueness and his maddening omissions for the sake of what he has saved. When he wrote, in the twilight days of Athens, Greece was a Roman province, and much of what he has to say is influenced by Roman manners. He gives us the names of the great gourmets of the past and anecdotes about them, but he never manages to complete a recipe, even when he does begin to give one in the course of a story; what actually went on in the kitchen is more of a mystery to him than the reasons why a cook is so expensive. And he is often more interested in the medical effect of a particular kind of food than its use in cookery. This attitude, which reflects the central place that theories of diet held in Greek medicine, will recur in many later writers, with the result that we know more about the ingredients of classical and medieval cookery than about the end-products.

Athenaeus begins his book with the intention of using the dinner as a literary framework and of describing the meal as well as the conversation. Though he abandons his scheme at the main course, there are long lists of possible foods for the earlier part of the dinner. An Athenian *hors d'œuvre* sounds quite familiar even if the contents are not: 'the cook sets before you a large tray on which are five small plates. One of these holds garlic, another a pair of sea-urchins, another a sweet wine sop, another ten cockles, the last a small piece of sturgeon.' Sturgeon was a delicacy down to the end of the Middle Ages, and is still a royal fish in Britain: any sturgeon taken in British waters is regarded as the monarch's property. Cockles, on the other hand, are much underrated today; both Greeks and Romans prized them, particularly the smooth-shelled variety which are a kind of small clam. Another possible ingredient of this *propome* or appetizer course sounds much stranger to our ears, namely bulbs. These were a traditional dish. The poet Hesiod in the sixth century B.C. praised asphodel bulbs pounded with figs as a delicacy, while Pliny, writing his *Natural History* in Italy six hundred years later, mentions gladiolus bulbs boiled and eaten with bread, as well as six different varieties to which the Greeks were partial. He adds instructions on how to gather bulbs:

Bulbs are dug up before the beginning of spring, or else they at once go off in quality; it is a sign that they are ripe when the leaves become dry at the lower end. The rather green ones are disapproved of, as also are the long and the small ones, whereas those of a reddish colour and rounder shape are praised, as are those of the largest size. Usually their top has a better taste and the middle parts are sweet.

Perhaps this traditional dish goes back in time to the primitive days when food was difficult to store and the end of winter was a period of great scarcity; anything that was edible then, let alone at its best, would have been much sought after.

Athenaeus also gives us an exhaustive list of fish, among which the favourites in classical times were eels and lampreys, two dishes which we have almost forgotten. On the other hand, lobsters put in only a very brief appearance, and large prawns were much preferred. Squid, octopus and cuttlefish, still staple Mediterranean fare, are there; boiled squid stuffed with minced meat is mentioned in a Greek comedy. Unfortunately it is at the meat course that Athenaeus abandons his scheme of debating each course of the dinner as it appears. He serves his guests with hams and mustard, and then dismisses the rest of the meal, saying:

Although many viands of all kinds were brought in successively after these we shall indicate only those which deserve record. For beside a quantity of other birds, including geese, there were also the small birds which some call woodpeckers, also pigs and the much sought-after pheasants.

Disappointingly, when he does give us a recipe, it turns out to come from the pages of the one Roman cookery book which has survived.

Athenaeus on the whole tends to philosophize to little purpose. A much more rewarding figure, though equally remote from the realities of the kitchen, is Epicurus, whose teachings have given us the idea of an epicure and of an epicurean feast. Not that Epicurus's own philosophy was as simple as the phrase by which it is usually summed up – 'Gather ye rosebuds while ye may'. Epicurus himself denied on scientific grounds that the gods had any moral functions if they existed at all, and he deduced from the absence of any after-life or system of divine rewards and punishments that the best man could expect from life was an existence of undisturbed peace and tranquillity. He would have been horrified at the way in which his name was invoked by gluttons feverishly searching for new pleasures, for it was only his disciples who invoked his maxim that pleasure appeared to be the root of all good and based their ideas on it. The senses were regarded by them as all-important and to be indulged to the full: Metrodorus, a close friend of the philosopher, is supposed to have said, 'It is our business, not to seek crowns by saving the Greeks, but to enjoy ourselves in good eating and drinking.' Epicurus had stressed the avoidance of excitement or passion, to the extent of avoiding marriage. Now his teaching was invoked by those who pursued both, and particularly by the new lords of Greece, the Romans, whose military exploits in the East had brought them into contact with new luxuries on which to squander the wealth of an empire. So Epicurus deserves his place in the history of cookery, but he is present, so to speak, in disguise. A more suitable patron saint would have been the now shadowy figure of Archestratus the Sicilian, who in the fourth century B.C. is said to have scoured the world for new dishes, and who – by his own account – was the first to invent 'artificial' dishes, where flavours which did not occur together in nature were blended by the cook's art.

From these scanty pickings from the larder of the Greeks we turn more hopefully to the Roman tradition. Like so much else in Roman civilization, Roman cookery consists of a simple native basis, rustic and unpolished, overlaid with Greek and Oriental sophistication. The attitude of early Rome to luxury was hostile, and Stoic or Spartan ideals would have found a readier audience than Epicurus's followers. The Republican period in Rome which ended with Augustus's rise to imperial power in 27 B.C. saw the passing of various edicts restricting private luxury, such as the Lex Fannia of 161 B.C. which limited the number of guests at anyone's table to three, with two extra allowed on market days, and prohibited the eating of shellfish, dormice and 'strange birds brought from another world'. The maximum amount that could be spent on food was also fixed, as if the legislators anticipated the excesses of the years to come. Augustus himself continued the tradition of austerity, as Suetonius tells us: 'He was frugal, and, as a rule, preferred the food of the common people, especially the coarser sort of bread, whitebait, fresh hand-pressed cheese, and green figs of the second crop; and would not wait for dinner, if he felt hungry, but ate anywhere.' Even in more lavish surroundings a hint of the ancient simplicity remained: Horace, writing under Augustus's reign, speaks of a meal as lasting '*ab ovo ad malum*' (from the egg to the apple), and an egg dish remained the traditional opening course of a feast.

But the seeds of luxury had already been sown by Augustus's time. The historian Livy marked the year 168 B.C. as the moment when the ancient Roman virtues were first assailed by eastern vices:

It was through the army serving in Asia (which had just overthrown the Macedonian kingdom) that the beginnings of foreign luxury were introduced into the City. These men brought into Rome for the first time bronze couches, costly coverlets, tapestry and other fabrics, and what was at that time considered gorgeous furniture – pedestal tables and silver salvers. Banquets were made more attractive by the presence of girls who played on the harp and sang and danced, and by other forms of amusement, and the banquets themselves began to be prepared with greater care and expense. The cook whom the ancients regarded and treated as the lowest menial was rising in value, and what had been a servile office came to be looked upon as a fine art. Still, what met the eye in those days was hardly the germs of the luxury that was coming.

So just as Alexander's men were reputed, though perhaps with less justice, to have brought back strange novelties from their victorious foray into India a century and a half before, the East was now blamed once more as the source of degenerate habits.

This was far from the whole truth. Plautus, whose plays are the earliest surviving pieces in Roman literature, has some pungent remarks to make about cooks well before this. There is a biting scene in one comedy in which a citizen hires a cook and finds that he has taken on more than he bargained for. According to the cook:

I am a man who seasons a dinner differently from other cooks, who season me whole plantations and put 'em on platters and make oxen out of guests, pile on the fodder, and then proceed to season that fodder with more fodder. They serve them sorrel, cabbage, beets, spinach, flavoured with coriander, fennel, garlic, parsley, pour in a pound of asafoetida, grate in murderous mustard that makes the graters' eyes ooze out before they have it grated. When these chaps season the dinners that they come and cook, they use for seasoning no seasonings, but screech-owls, to eat the entrails out of living guests. This explains why people here have such short lives – filling their bellies full of fodder of this sort, ghastly to mention, let alone to eat. Fodder that cattle will not eat, men eat nowadays . . . Why, those that fare on food that I have seasoned are enabled to live as much as two hundred years. Why, when I have put a dash of cinnatopsis in the pans, or clovitopsis, or sageolio, or allspiceria, they heat up automatically and instantaneously. These are my seasonings for Neptune's cattle: terrestrial cattle I season with cassitopsis, pepitilis or capsicoria.

Roman comedy, like Roman cookery, owed much to Greece, and Plautus may have been adapting a Greek play, but the butt of his satire must have been familiar to Roman audiences, or the scene would be pointless. The spices are of course all inventions, fancy names with a faint echo of reality. Plautus's successor Terence coined a phrase which became proverbial when he described a man's dinners as *cenae dubiae*, dinners of doubt, because they were all served at once and so varied that the bewildered guest did not know where to begin. He was probably thinking of a meal like that served by the senator Metellus in the middle years of the Republic, long before such luxury was commonplace. The first course, or *ante coenum*, comprised shellfish, sea-urchins, oysters, grape-fed fieldfares and asparagus; the first main course included shellfish again, clams, stewed oysters and fatted fowls, and was followed by a second main course of mussels, purple murex and other shellfish, figpeckers, cutlets of wild goat and boar, chicken pie and snipe. The guests were then confronted by sows' wombs, boar's head, stewed fish, stewed sows' hearts, ducks, boiled truffles, hares, roast fowls, bread sauce and a kind of sponge cake before they were allowed to relax their energies over a simple dessert.

Under Augustus, despite the emperor's own simple tastes, such extravaganzas were rife. Horace satirizes them as not only vulgar and wasteful but also dangerous to health:

For how harmful to a man a variety of dishes is, you may realize, if you recall that plain fare which agreed with you in other days. But as soon as you mix boiled and roast, shellfish and thrushes, the sweet will turn to bile, and the thick bile will cause intestine feud. Do you see how pale each guest rises from his *cena dubia*?

He was even more scathing in another satire about the new breed of cooks who regarded themselves as heralds of the 'new learning'. Meeting his friend Catius in the street, he asks the reason for his haste. 'I must get home to write down the marvellous lecture I've just heard,' cries Catius, and proceeds to recite a series of half-baked hints on cookery as though they were pearls of wisdom, continuing:

It is not everyone that may lightly claim skill in the dining art, without first mastering the subtle theory of flavours. Nor is it enough to sweep up fish from the expensive stall, not knowing which are better with sauce, and which, if broiled, will tempt the tired guests to raise himself once more upon his elbow . . .

Some there are whose talent lies only in finding new sweets; 'tis by no means enough to spend all one's care on a single point – just as if some-one were anxious only that his wines be good, and cared not what sauce he poured upon his fish.

The results of this high-sounding learning in the kitchen were often disastrous at the dinner table. It is Horace once again who paints the sorry picture of a dinner given by the wealthy Nasidienus, where each dish is accompanied by a lecture from the host, and strange concoctions overwhelm the guests. His longwindedness is repaid in kind, for two of his guests decide to 'drink him bank-rupt'; what worries him, however, is not the expense, but the danger that they will ruin their palates for the next delicacy. An ancient canopy which bedecks the room collapses on the guests, and when their host tries to make amends with new delights for the palate, he cannot restrain his loquaciousness, and the diners take flight, 'revenging ourselves by tasting nothing'.

Perhaps this should serve as a dire warning to modern experi-menters, for it is tempting to expound on curious dishes. This was the failing of one amateur of classical cookery in eighteenth-century fiction, the learned doctor who offers the hero of Smollett's novel *Peregrine Pickle* a dinner in the antique Roman style. Smollett had studied his Roman cookery in the edition of Apicius's cookery book – to which we shall shortly come – produced by Martin Lister, Queen Anne's personal physician. His menu is authentic enough, while the doctor proves to be a latter-day Nasidienus indeed, but the effect on his guests is not quite what the host expected:

The painter, who had by wry faces, testify'd his abhorrence of the sow's stomach, which he compared to a bagpipe, and the snails which had undergone purgation, no sooner heard him mention the roasted pullets, than he eagerly sollicited a wing of the fowl; upon which the doctor desired he would take the trouble of cutting them up, and accordingly sent them round, while Mr Pallet tucked the table-cloth under his chin, and brandished his knife and fork with singular address: but scarce were they set down before him, when tears ran down his cheeks, and he called aloud, in manifest disorder, 'Z——ds! This is the essence of a whole bed of garlic!' That he might not, however, dis-appoint or disgrace the entertainer, he applied his instruments to one of the birds, and when he opened up the cavity, was assaulted by such an irruption of intolerable smells, that without staying to disengage himself from the cloth, he sprung away, with an exclamation of, 'Lord Jesus!' and involved the whole table in havock, ruin and confusion.

As an antidote to Smollett's cheerful exaggerations, let us return to some earlier Roman dinner tables. Dinner parties were small, rarely more than nine guests; women were excluded. The guests and their host reclined on couches surrounding three sides of a table. Later the table became round, and the furnishings could be enlarged to any size required, and by the end of the first century A.D. it was occasionally a half-moon shape. The dishes were placed on the open side of the table, but each guest had an attendant who would fill his cup and act as waiter. The main meal was at midday, and was very much a social occasion at which great men would display their wealth and repay their hangers-on by an invitation. Here is another satirist, Juvenal, on the woes of an unfortunate diner-out of the latter ilk. (Incidentally, if our view of Roman dining seems particularly full of malicious portraits and disastrous meals, it is simply because it is only the satirists who give us these insights into daily life; but their lively distortions are often better than an accurate but prosaic record.)

> Get one thing clear from the start: a dinner-invitation
> Settles the score in full for all your earlier
> Services. This great 'friendship' produces—food. Each meal,
> However infrequent, your patron reckons against you
> To square his accounts. So if, after two months' neglect,
> With the bottom place to be filled at the lowest table,
> He says 'Be my guest' to you, his forgotten retainer,
> You're beside yourself with joy. What more could Trebius
> Hope for? . . .
>
>   Yet – heavens! – what a dinner!
> The wine's so rough sheep-clippings wouldn't absorb it,
> And turns the guests into raving madmen. At first
> It's only insults – but soon a regular battle
> Breaks out between you and the freedmen, cheap crockery flies
> In all directions, you're slinging cups yourself
> And mopping the blood off with a crimsoned table-napkin.
> The wine that Virro, your host, is drinking has lain in its bottle

Since the consuls wore long hair: those grapes were trodden
During the Social Wars – yet never a glassful
Will he send to a friend with heartburn . . .

My lord will have his mullet, imported from Corsica or from
The rocks below Taormina: home waters are all fished out
To fill such ravening maws, our local breeding grounds
Are trawled without cease, the market never lets up –
We kill off the fry now, close seasons go by the board.
Today we import from abroad for domestic consumption: these
Are the luxury fish which legacy-hunters purchase,
And which their spinster quarries sell back to the retailer.
Virro is served with a lamprey; no finer specimen
Ever came from Sicilian waters. When the south wind lies low,
Drying damp wings in his cell, then hardy fishermen
Will dare the wrath of the Straits. But what's in store for you?
An eel, perhaps (though it looks like a water-snake), or
A grey-mottled river-pike, born and bred in the Tiber,
Bloated with sewage, a regular visitor to
The cesspools underlying the slums of the Subura.

. . . Meanwhile, to ensure that
No cause for resentment is lacking, behold the carver
Prancing about, with flourishes of his knife,
Obedient to all his master's instructions: no
Small matter to make a nice distinction between the
Carving of hares and hens!

We shall meet the carver and his flourishes again; but most of
Juvenal's wit is barbed against purely Roman outrageousness.
Mullet, as he indicates, were prized above all other delicacies, and
he had already pilloried the knight Crispinus for buying a red
mullet for sixty gold pieces, imagining that if things went on like
that, the emperor would soon be summoning his entire cabinet to
ponder how to cook a giant turbot which had just been presented
to him. And indeed the excesses of the Roman rulers scarcely fell
short of that. Vitellius is described by Suetonius as ruled by gluttony
and cruelty:

He banqueted three and often four times a day, namely morning,
noon, afternoon, and evening – the last meal being mainly a drinking
bout – and survived the ordeal well enough by taking frequent emetics.

What made things worse was that he used to invite himself out to private banquets at all hours; and these never cost his various hosts less than 4000 gold pieces each. The most notorious feast of the series was given him by his brother on his entry into Rome; 2000 magnificent fish and 7000 game birds are said to have been served. Yet even this hardly compares in luxuriousness with a single tremendously large dish which Vitellius dedicated to the Goddess Minerva and named 'Shield of Minerva the Protectress'. The recipe called for pike-livers, pheasant brains, peacock brains, flamingo tongues and lamprey-milt; and the ingredients, collected in every corner of the Empire from the Parthian frontier to the Straits of Gibraltar, were brought to Rome by naval triremes.

Elagabalus in the early third century attempted to outdo all his predecessors by offering his guests phoenix, but had to be content with ostriches' brains. He it was who heaped enormous rewards on the inventors of new sauces, and would eat shellfish only at enormous distances from the sea to make them as costly as possible. Gibbon says of him that he:

abandoned himself to the grossest pleasures with ungoverned fury, and soon found disgust and satiety in the midst of his enjoyments. The inflammatory powers of art were summoned to his aid: the confused multitudes of women, of wines, and of dishes, and the studied variety of attitudes and sauces, served to revive his languid appetites. New terms and new inventions in these sciences, the only ones cultivated and patronized by the monarch, signalized his reign, and transmitted his infamy to succeeding times.

It is extravagances such as those of Nero or Vitellius that Petronius attacks in his account of the most famous of all Roman dinner parties, Trimalchio's supper in the *Satyricon*. Amidst all the talk, the food is like a series of spectacular fireworks, designed as much to keep the party going with ingenious tricks as to feed the guests. But Petronius is ridiculing the worst excesses of Roman gourmets, and what starts in a fairly unassuming style ends in a crescendo of laughable horrors. The first dish, black and green olives, accompanied by dormice in honey and poppy seed with sausages, is one for which recipes still survive. But thereafter fantasy takes over. The eggs served turn out to be made of pastry and to contain figpeckers, a bird which the Romans regarded as a great delicacy. Then follows a dish containing titbits appropriate to the signs of the zodiac engraved round its rim. Soon afterwards a hare 'with wings fixed to his middle to look like Pegasus' makes an appearance. A wild boar turns out to be stuffed with live thrushes, and when the chef is accused of forgetting to gut a pig, he slices it open at the table and blood-puddings and sausages tumble out. Cakes and apples are joke pastries, stuffed with saffron, and when the proper pastries follow they are in the shape of thrushes and are stuffed with raisins and nuts, while quinces are stuck with thorns to make them look like sea-urchins. The crowning masterpiece is a fat goose surrounded by fish and all kinds of game – which turns out to be made entirely of pork, and the host boasts that his chef will 'produce a fish out of a sow's belly, a pigeon out of the lard, a turtle dove out of the ham, and fowl out of the knuckle'. For the jaded palates of the guests the taste of the food has long since been forgotten; only appearances and trickery can excite their appetites, and in this Petronius underlines the absence of visual appeal in ordinary Roman cookery. Because it is such a spectacular description, Trimalchio's dinner has become a set-piece which is always quoted to illustrate a Roman feast; but it is really an eccentric piece of comedy.

Our menu, however, will not be constructed on such uneasy foundations. Instead, Pliny's old-fashioned Roman dinner of 'single lettuces, triple snails, twin eggs, barley wine with honey, sweet wine and snow, Boeotian olives, cucumbers, bulbs and a thousand other things, all just as splendid' will be our guide, though since many of the recipes come from more luxurious times, its ingredients will come from the farthest ends of the Empire: oysters from Colchester, hams, pork and sausages from Gaul, Belgian and Westphalian hams, asparagus from Rheims, Libyan prawns, cinnamon from Arabia, spices from lands beyond even the Empire's borders. From nearer to Rome, there will be Greek olives and the native Italian pork which was 'a passion of the Roman palate'. Not for us the excessive niceties of mullet cooked in a glass vessel before the guests, changing hue as it died, lampreys made sweeter by feeding them on slaves or even fig-fattened pigs, killed with draughts of wine and honey; for what we know about Roman cookery is essentially what a citizen's household might have eaten. There are some luxuries and recipes which are clearly too elaborate for everyday use, but although the one surviving cookery book bears the name of a famous gourmet, it contains largely bourgeois cuisine.

The work which goes under the title of *Apicius on the Art of Cooking; in Ten Books* is almost certainly a late compilation of the fourth or fifth century A.D. The man whose name is given as author, M. Gabius Apicius, lived under the reign of Tiberius, in the first century A.D. Many stories were told about his gastronomic exploits, and Seneca relates his last incredible gesture: finding that he had only ten million sesterces left of a fortune which had once been ten times as great – the difference having been squandered on food – he committed suicide on the grounds that no true gourmet could be expected to exist on a pittance of that sort. Many devices and discoveries about food were attributed to him, such as the fig-fed and wine-slaughtered pigs already mentioned, and his name was a byword. Seneca also tells the story of the mullet weighing four and a half pounds which was presented to Tiberius:

Tiberius ordered it to be sent to the fish-market and put up for sale, remarking: 'I shall be taken entirely by surprise, my friends, if either Apicius or P. Octavius does not buy that mullet.' The guess came true beyond his expectation: the two men bid, and Octavius won, thereby acquiring a great reputation among his intimates because he had bought for five thousand sesterces a fish which the Emperor had sold, and which even Apicius did not succeed in buying.

Apicius is said to have written two works, one on cookery in general, the other on sauces, and parts of both of these, combined with borrowings from humbler works on basic cookery and occasional recipes named after great gourmets, make up the collection that has come down to us.

From the descriptions of dinners already quoted, and from the 'artificial' attitude towards cooking of both Greeks and Romans, it is hardly surprising that the dishes which are probably Apicius's own rarely present the food in its natural form, and usually aim at disguising both original ingredients and method in a subtle blend of spices. Apicius's motto might well be his own proud boast at the end of an 'anchovy pâté without anchovies' that 'at table no one will know what he is eating'. Judging by the appearance of many Roman dishes, there was no great concern with aesthetic pleasure for the eye; a reasonable test of whether a Roman recipe is completed is the universal greyness that seems to pervade their food, combined with a liking for pâtés, minced meat and omelette-like dishes, of which Seneca wrote scathingly: 'I expect they will soon be put on the table ready chewed for us, for there is very little difference between so doing and what the cook does now.'

The other accusation which has often been levelled against Roman cookery in recent times is substantially Smollett's complaint: it is full of unfamiliar spices used in enormous quantities. Anyone who has tried the recipes will at once realize how untrue this is. For all their love of ostentation and the poets' endless satires on the jaded palates of the great gourmets, the Romans would never have persisted with such a diet. Nor is their method of preparing food particularly close to that practised in the Far East today: curries are much more pungent, and rely on a bland base such as rice or the accompanying side-dishes of a *rijstaafel* for their effect. The misunderstanding seems to have arisen because Roman recipes very rarely specify quantities, and when they do, it is on a scale far beyond that of the modern recipe books, where the portions are rarely designed for more than eight people. So the true aroma of a Roman dinner should be perfumed rather than penetrating, and the multitude of spices should be used with caution, to produce a subtle blend that reveals the cook's skill rather than an overpowering odour.

With this in mind, let us turn to the recipes themselves. The original text is often obscure, and what follows are interpretations rather than literal transcriptions.

Basic requirements
Equipment

The Roman kitchen utensils were not greatly different from those we use today. Saucepans, frying pans, ladles, strainers and dishes were all fairly similar in appearance to modern ones. The cooking pot, much used for boiling joints of meat or making basic porridge-like dishes, had less of a place in a wealthy man's kitchen than in the barracks or in a country kitchen. Cooking was done over a hearth, often on charcoal or occasionally on wood with a special aroma, such as cypress; there was no easy means of regulating heat, and ovens were not widely used for this reason, though a variety of kinds did exist.

In terms of the modern kitchen, the biggest difference is the absence of slave labour to carry out the endless pounding and puréeing of dishes. Almost every recipe requires the use of a pestle and mortar. Those who wish to avoid this often strenuous work can get round it by the use of a liquidizer and coffer grinder attachment* – which are after all our modern equivalent of slaves. I have included their use in the recipes where appropriate, but the coffee grinder can be employed to avoid pounding spices. As each different type of spice or herb is bought, it should be finely ground and stored in powder form. This allows much greater accuracy in measuring out for recipes; but purists are welcome to stick to the pestle and mortar. It is worth remembering that the addition of a little liquid in the mortar before the spice or herbs are added to the rest of the dish will prevent wastage when only small amounts are being pounded.

Ingredients

A good supply of olive oil and cooking wine (red) is essential. The Romans never used butter, so instructions to fry or grill always mean the use of oil. The wine should preferably be Italian, but of reasonable quality. The other important liquid ingredients are unsweetened white grape juice, which is usually available in bottles from health food stores, and is a passable substitute for fresh grape juice, and the basic Roman seasoning called *liquamen* or *garum*. Both of these need preparation.

The unsweetened grape juice is always reduced by boiling to thicken it, and its various degrees of thickness have different names. Rather than confuse the issue by using the Roman terms, I

---

* Or with a mincer, which avoids uniform smoothness of texture in meat and vegetable recipes.

have simply indicated the appropriate procedure under each recipe. For those who are interested, *defrutum* is only slightly reduced, *caroenum* has been reduced by one third in volume, and *sapa* has been reduced by two thirds of its volume.

Liquamen or *garum* has been a source of controversy for a long while. It is basically a form of salt solution, flavoured with fish, and used instead of salt, which appears in only a handful of recipes in its powdered form. It is only very remotely like Worcester sauce, to which modern writers often compare it. The biggest difficulty in using it is that wide variations in strength occur with the use of different methods. Quantities should therefore be treated with caution in the recipes themselves; just as a modern cook decides how much salt to use, so the Roman cook would adjust his seasoning with *liquamen*. The following method will produce a strongly salt solution, with only a slight flavour of fish, to be used sparingly:

¾ *pint water*	*1 lb whitebait, sprats*
3 oz salt	*or sardines (fresh)*
tsp ground origan	

Dissolve salt in water, and stir in origan. Add fish and bring to the boil, stirring continuously. Boil for two to three minutes. Strain first through sieve, and then pour resulting liquid two or three times through muslin until free of sediment. Bottle and cork securely.

Liquamen was usually produced on a large scale, and there were even factories for it in large towns. It was also a lengthy process, and the recipe given above is really a kind of 'instant' method. A method which comes closer to the standard procedure is as follows:

1 lb mackerel or sprats
salt

Split fish and roll in salt until thickly coated. Put in lowest possible oven, and allow to dry rather than cook; this will take about two days, and the oven should be turned off at intervals to reduce the temperature. The effect required is that of drying in the sun. When the fish are reasonably free of moisture, place them in a large sieve and pour one pint of boiling water over them. Take up the resulting liquid and repeat two or three times. Strain through muslin and bottle, sealing tightly. This will produce a less salty but more flavoured version.

Another important ingredient is honey. Although the Romans had heard of sugar, they regarded it as a curiosity to be found in the East, and made no attempt to import it. Honey was therefore their only method of sweetening, but they also used it in many of their sauces, usually in conjunction with pepper. The distinction between sweet and sour was less clearly defined than in our rather artificial division, and many sweetmeats were eaten with spices which we would regard as sharp, pepper again being the commonest example.

Many of the meat pâtés and 'made dishes', as the seventeenth-century cooks would have called them, have a basis of calves' brains. These are not easy to obtain today, since they have to be fresh, and there is little demand for them. The best substitute is sweetbreads, though these have a more positive flavour which makes them less suitable as a base. I have therefore specified 'sweetbreads or brains' wherever the original recipe gives brains; if sweetbreads are given alone, this means that they are in the original. Sweetbreads should always be soaked for about three hours before cooking. They can, however, be bought already soaked and then only need a quick wash in cold water before blanching.

The following spices are common in Roman cookery, and will need to be obtained from a good health food shop or herbalist (Culpeper House Ltd, 21 Bruton Street, London W.1, will usually have supplies):

lovage root	tansy
pennyroyal	celery seed
dill	rue
savory	origan
cumin	fenugreek

Of these, the most essential are lovage and pennyroyal; it is advisable to check the recipes carefully before starting to see whether any others are required.

The other problematical ingredient is pine-kernels. These were used in large quantities, rather as medieval cooks were to use blanched almonds, as a basis for sauces and in pâtés. They are not only difficult to obtain, but also expensive (£1.60 per lb at 1973 prices); however, theycan be found in health food shops and Italian delicatessens. Almonds are probably the best substitute, though on the bitter side, whereas pine-kernels are sweet; hazelnut-kernels would be a possible substitute, but it is a good idea to try to obtain at least a small quantity of the pine-kernels themselves for comparison with the substitutes. Neither almonds nor hazelnuts should be used in the same quantity as the pine-kernels, as their flavour is considerably stronger and will tend to 'come through' too much.

Roman Recipes

ISICIUM [for 2 persons]

A kind of soufflé omelette with brains or sweetbreads.

1 lb sweetbreads or brains
¼ pt liquamen, diluted with
  ¼ pt water
2 oz dry pastry crumbs
¼ tsp lovage root, ground

4 eggs
2 glasses red wine
¼ tsp pepper
½ tsp ground origan

Soak sweetbreads in cold water and blanch for 7–10 minutes; if using brains, remove fibres and blanch in same way. Blend pepper, lovage, and origan in *liquamen*. Put sweetbreads and one third of blended spices and *liquamen* in liquidizer, and add eggs. Beat until smooth, adding more *liquamen* if required. Cook in a very lightly oiled large omelette pan without stirring, over a very low fire, until completely set. Turn out onto a chopping board and cut into one inch squares.

Sauce
Take remainder of *liquamen* and spices, add red wine, and bring to the boil. Thicken by blending in pastry crumbs (a birch twig whisk is help-ful for this). Pour over squares of isicium, and sprinkle with pepper to taste.

SALACATTABIA APICIANA [for 6–8 persons]

A terrine of chicken and sweetbreads. This is a delicious recipe, and a very good introduction to Roman cookery. It shows up the different way in which the Romans used aromas rather than flavours to achieve a very subtle result.

1 cooked chicken
½ lb cheddar cheese*
1 sliced cucumber

1 tsp celery seed, ground
½ tsp dried mint
½ tsp ground coriander

* Vestine cheese was a mild hard cheese; ordinary cheddar is a good equivalent.

26

3 tsp honey
3 tbs oil
2–3 oz dried onions
2 lb sweetbreads
1 loaf pumpernickel
8 oz pine-kernels

1 tsp ground pennyroyal
¾ tsp ginger
4 oz seedless raisins
1 glass vinegar
1 glass red wine

A lightly oiled deep square-section mould is needed for this.

Slice the pumpernickel and line the mould with it. Soak the sweetbreads in cold water, drain and blanch for 7–10 minutes. Carve the chicken and break up into small pieces. Fill the mould with the ingredients in the following order: chicken, pine-kernels, chopped sweetbreads, cucumber, dried onions and coarsley chopped cheese.

Blend the herbs, spices, oil, vinegar, honey and red wine, stir in the raisons, and pour over the filled mould. Place the mould in a baking tray full of hot water, and cover with silver foil. Cook in the oven at Regulo Mark 4 (340°) for 25–30 minutes. The cheese should melt and bind the mixture together; it should be placed in the refrigerator to set, and then turned out. Serve slightly chilled.

EVERYDAY PATINA [for 2 persons]

¾ lb sweetbreads or brains
¼ pt milk
5 tbs unsweetened grape juice

3 tbs liquamen
2 eggs
¼ tsp cumin seed

Soak sweetbreads in cold water, drain and blanch for 7–10 minutes. Prepare grape juice by bringing to boil and reducing by one third. Blend ground cumin seed and liquamen. Put sweetbreads, grape juice, cumin seed, *liquamen*, milk and eggs in liquidizer and beat unil smooth. Put in a shallow earthenware dish and place in a baking tray full of hot water in a low oven (Regulo Mark 2–3, 300–320°) until set, about 45 minutes.

MINUTAL APICIUS [for 4 persons]

A kind of fricassee.

1 lb sausage meat
½ lb whitebait
1 lb sweetbreads
2 leeks
6 tbs liquamen
2 glasses wine
½ tps dried mint or fresh mint sprig

Sauce
½ tsp pepper
½ tsp ground lovage root
1 tsp ground coriander
1 tsp honey

Soak sweetbreads in cold water. Wash, chop and part-cook leeks in oil. Add sausage meat, whitebait and drained sweetbreads to leeks, together with mint, *liquamen* and wine. Simmer until all the meat is thoroughly cooked.

Blend spices and *liquamen* with honey. Add the liquamen, spices and honey to the meat, and stir in well before serving.

CHICKEN À LA VARIUS   [For 4 persons]

Chicken in a light white sauce.

3 lb chicken	Sauce
2 tbs liquamen	*¼ tsp pepper*
½ glass red wine	*2 oz pine-kernels*
3 tbs oil	*5 tbs liquamen*
Bouquet: chopped leek,	*6 tbs strained stock*
½ tsp coriander, ¼ tsp savory	*¼ pt milk*
	Whites of 2 eggs

Cook the chicken in a casserole with the *liquamen*, wine, oil and bouquet in a moderate oven (Regulo Mark 5, 360°) for 50 minutes. Remove chicken from liquid and place in fireproof serving dish in low oven to keep warm.

Strain liquid, and retain about ¼ pt for sauce. Pound pine-kernels, add pepper, *liquamen* and stock, and blend with milk in liquidizer. Beat egg whites until just stiff. Put contents of liquidizer in saucepan, and bring to boil. Remove from fire and stir in egg whites, ensuring that no lumps form. Pour over chicken and serve.

CHICKEN À LA FRONTO   [for 4 persons]

This recipe relies on cooking the chicken in herbs to give the meat a fragrant flavour.

3 lb chicken	*½ tsp dill*
3 tbs oil	*½ leek*
2 tbs liquamen	*¼ tsp coriander*
2 glasses unsweetened grape juice	*½ tsp savory*

Brown the chicken in half the oil in a casserole. Blend the herbs with the *liquamen* and the rest of the oil, and pour over the chicken. Cook in a moderate oven (Regulo Mark 5, 360°) for 50 minutes. Remove chicken from liquid. Meanwhile, reduce the grape juice by one third by boiling. Pour this over the chicken, and sprinkle with pepper before serving.

ALEXANDRIAN GRILLED FISH   [for 4 persons]

This sauce can be used with a variety of white fish; in this version it is a kind of forerunner of Sole Véronique, with a typically Roman base to the sauce instead of the béchamel, producing an aromatic rather than a bland result.

4 lemon soles

Sauce
4 oz (seedless) raisins	*1 glass red wine*
½ tsp pepper	*5 tbs oil*
½ tsp ground lovage	*2–3 tbs liquamen*
1 tsp ground coriander	*1 glass sweet white wine*
	or *4 tsp honey*

Clean the lemon soles, and brush lightly with oil. Grill under a hot grill until just brown. Put aside in a covered dish to keep warm.

Blend pepper, lovage and coriander in *liquamen*. Put in a medium saucepan. Add oil, red wine, white wine (or honey) and whole raisins. Bring the sauce slowly up to just below boiling point, stirring well. Pour over the soles and serve.

PEAS À LA VITELLIUS

Vegetables were rarely presented in their natural form, but had to be disguised. This is a typical treatment of dried peas, where there was some justification for 'dressing up'.

8 oz peas, preferably dried	*1 tbs liquamen*
*2 yolks of hard-boiled eggs**	*1 dsp wine vinegar*
1 tsp honey	*⅛ tsp pepper*
1 tbs oil	*¼ tsp ground lovage*
1 tbs red wine	*⅛ tsp powdered ginger*

If the peas are dried, soak them overnight. Cook the peas in ¾ pt water until thoroughly soft. Make into a purée by sieving them with a little of the cooking water.

Blend pepper, ginger and lovage in a small saucepan with the wine, *liquamen* and vinegar. Add the oil, and bring the mixture to the boil. When it boils, take it off the flame and blend with the peas. Add honey to taste and serve.

* The whites of the hard-boiled eggs can be chopped and used as decoration, though this is not in the original.

A DRESSING FOR CUCUMBER

Roman salad dressings differ little from ours in their basic ingredients, but use far more herbs. This is unusual in relying on just one herb for its character.

3 peppercorns
½ tsp pennyroyal, ground or
pounded as finely as possible

1 tsp honey
3 tbs liquamen
1 tbs vinegar (wine)

Pound peppercorns and pennyroyal in mortar. Add, in the mortar, honey, *liquamen* and vinegar, and blend thoroughly. This should be sufficient for a medium-sized sliced cucumber.

TURNIPS

Turnips might seem a surprising dish to find at a Roman dinner, but in the absence of potatoes they were prized as a base for sauces which had no predominant flavour of their own. Imitation anchovies were reputedly made from pickled turnips.

4 medium-sized turnips
½ tsp cumin
1 tsp honey
pinch of rue

5 tbs grape juice for defrutum
5 tbs liquamen
2 tbs oil
1 tbs vinegar

Prepare *defrutum* by bringing the grape juice to the boil and reducing by one third. Boil the turnips until just soft (15–20 minutes), drain and cut into quarters. Place in a serving dish and keep warm. Pound the cumin and rue and add *liquamen* in the mortar; if already ground, add to *defrutum* with *liquamen* and blend. Add vinegar, honey and oil to mixture of spices, *liquamen* and *defrutum*, and bring to the boil. As soon as the mixture comes to the boil, withdraw from flame and pour over turnips.

PEAS

This recipe is best done with young peas, either fresh or deep-frozen.

1 lb peas
1 leek, finely chopped
2 tbs liquamen
1 glass wine
½ pt water

½ tsp cumin
½ tsp coriander
¼ tsp lovage
½ tsp pepper
tsp basil

} *all ground*

Boil the peas in unsalted water. When cooked add the leek, coriander and cumin. Blend the lovage, pepper, basil, *liquamen* and wine, and add to the peas. Bring to the boil again and simmer for 10 minutes, stirring occasionally.

CABBAGE

This is a similar treatment to the recipe for peas given above, and again young cabbages should be used.

1 young cabbage	*2 leeks*
1 tbs liquamen	*1 tbs red wine*
2 tbs oil	*¾ tsp ground cumin*
¼ tsp pepper	*¼ tsp ground coriander*
½ tsp caraway seed, ground	

Quarter and cook the cabbage until just tender in unsalted water. Drain, and reserve the water. Cut away the stalk and dice the leaves. Chop half of one leek. Boil the remaining one and a half leeks in the water from the cabbage. Make a dressing of oil, *liquamen*, wine and cumin. Add the pepper, caraway and coriander to the chopped raw leek. Arrange in a serving dish with the boiled leeks halved at the bottom, then the cabbage, and finally the chopped spiced raw leek.

LEEKS

A simple but effective combination of slightly unlikely ingredients.

1 lb leeks	*4 oz green olives*
2 tbs oil	*1 tbs liquamen*
¼ pt salted water	*1 tbs wine*

Stone olives and chop. Cut leeks into rounds and simmer with the olives in half the oil and the water for 15 minutes. Mix remaining oil, *liquamen* and wine as a dressing, and pour over the leeks before serving.

CELERY

This is one of the few recipes where attention is paid to the appearance of the dish: the cooking soda is intended to keep the celery green.

1 lb celery	*½ tsp cooking soda*
1 small onion	*¼ tsp pepper*
1 tbs wine	*¾ tsp origan*
1½ tbs oil	*½ tbs liquamen*

Boil the celery in cooking soda and water until tender. Drain and chop finely. Mix the remaining ingredients in the liquidizer. Cook the mixture separately in a small saucepan, simmering for 5–6 minutes, and blend with the chopped celery.

MUSSEL SAUSAGE   [for 6 persons]

The Roman love of pounded and puréed food extended to *isicia* or coarse sausages. This recipe retains the flavour of the mussels but enriches them and changes their texture.

4 qts mussels	*4 oz pine-kernels*
6 oz wheat germ	*2 glasses white wine*
2 eggs	*Sausage skin*
3 tbs liquamen	*¾ tsp pepper*

Clean the mussels in cold water and throw out any that are broken or open; rinse several times. Stew until they open and throw out any that remain closed. Shell them and pound through a sieve to remove the sinews. Put the pounded mussels in a liquidizer with the wheat germ, eggs, pepper and half the *liquamen*. Stuff the sausage skin with this mixture, adding the pine-kernels (lightly chopped), and place under a slow grill until just brown. Blend remaining *liquamen* and wine, and bring to the boil, serve this as a sauce.

SAUCE FOR SCAMPI OR PRAWNS

A rich, slightly curry-flavoured sauce to go with boiled scampi or prawns.

1 small onion	*2 oz chopped dates*
2 tsp honey	*⅛ tsp pepper*
2 tbs white wine	*¼ tsp ground lovage*
2 tbs vinegar	*¼ tsp ground caraway*
2 tbs liquamen	*¾ tsp ground cumin*
1 tbs oil	*5 tbs grape juice*

Chop the onion and brown in oil. Put the grape juice in a small saucepan and bring to the boil; reduce by one third by boiling. Put the remaining ingredients into a liquidizer and add the grape juice. Blend, add to the browned onion and allow to thicken. Pour over the boiled shellfish, and serve with French or German mustard.

PATELLA OF FISH   [for 4 persons]

A smoked or cured fish is the basis for this variegated dish. The Romans did not hesitate to mix fish and meat, as in the *Minutal Apicius* given earlier.

½ *lb smoked haddock fillets*	*4 eggs*
½ *lb sweetbreads*	½ *lb chicken livers*
¾ *lb soft cream cheese*	¼ *tsp pepper*
¼ *tsp ground lovage*	½ *tsp ground origan*
½ *tsp chopped rue*	*2 tbs wine*
3 tbs oil	*2 tsp honey*
½ *tsp ground cumin*	

Soak the sweetbreads. Cook the haddock in oil until the flakes begin to separate. Hard-boil two of the eggs, and put the sweetbreads to blanch for 6–7 minutes. Dice the cooked haddock, hard-boiled eggs, sweetbreads and raw chicken livers. Add the cheese, wine, oil, honey and all spices except the cumin and put the mixture in a shallow fire-proof dish. Allow to cook gently on a low flame until the chicken livers are thoroughly browned. Stir in two whole raw eggs, and continue to cook until the mixture binds slightly. Serve sprinkled with cumin.

LAMB TARPEIANUS   [for 4 persons]

2½ *lb leg of lamb*

Dressing

⅛ *tsp pepper*
¼ *tsp rue*
½ *chopped onion*
¼ *tsp savory*
¼ *tsp thyme*
1 tbs liquamen

Sauce

¼ *tsp savory*
½ *chopped onion*
¾ *tsp rue*
2 oz chopped dates
2 tbs liquamen
1 glass wine
2 glasses grape juice
6 tbs oil

Blend the ingredients of the dressing together, and rub over the joint before roasting. Place the joint in an open pan with a little oil in the bottom, and cook for 60–70 minutes in a moderate oven (Regulo Mark 4, 340°).

Reduce the grape juice by boiling to two thirds of its original volume. Pour the rest of the ingredients into a liquidizer and add the grape juice. Blend and pour into a shallow pan. Bring to the boil and simmer until reduced to a thick consistency. Serve as a sauce to accompany the joint.

CONCHICLA [for 6 persons]

This is a fairly bland dish, designed to be eaten without accompanying vegetables.

2½ *lb chicken*	*1 lb sweetbreads*
1 lb peas	*2 tbs liquamen*
½ *glass wine*	*2 onions*
3 tbs oil	¾ *tsp coriander*
½ *tsp cumin*	¼ *tsp pepper*
4 oz pine-kernel	*6 eggs*

Soak the sweetbreads in cold water, blanch for 7 minutes. Cook the chicken in a covered casserole with the oil, *liquamen* and wine. Chop the onions and the sweetbreads and add with the coriander to the chicken. Simmer gently until the chicken is cooked (about 45–50 minutes). Take out the chicken, onion and sweetbreads and reserve the stock. Bone the chicken, dice the meat and add to the onion and sweetbreads.

Beat the pepper, cumin and eggs together, and add the stock. Boil the peas and purée half of them. Reserve the remainder whole. Add the purée to the mixture of egg, stock and spices, and pour over the chicken in a large flat fireproof dish. Cook over a low flame until the eggs are done. When cooked garnish with the whole peas and the pine-kernels.

SAUCE FOR COLD MEAT OR BRAWN

A piquant alternative to chutney, somewhere between that and horse-radish sauce. It is excellent with brawn and other cold meats.

¼ *tsp pepper*	*2 oz broken cashew nuts*
¼ *tsp ground cumin*	*1 tbs honey*
¼ *tsp ground celery seed*	*1 tbs vinegar*
½ *oz finely chopped thyme*	*1 tbs liquamen*
2 oz pine-kernels	*4 tbs oil*

Blend the ingredients in a liquidizer, putting in the oil and nuts first, until it reaches a thick but not completely smooth consistency.

PATINA OF PEARS

A kind of sweet omelette; again, the Romans did not make the same distinction between fruit and vegetables, and this seems to have accompanied meat dishes on occasions.

$1\frac{1}{2}$ *lbs pears*	*2 tsp honey*
3 eggs	*2 tbs liquamen*
$\frac{1}{2}$ *glass sweet white wine*	*1 tbs oil*

Peel, core and slice pears. Put in liquidizer with honey, *liquamen*, wine and oil and blend. Pour into a fairly shallow pan, and simmer until the mixture thickens, draining off any surplus water from the pears. Stir in the beaten eggs and cook until they are done. Serve sprinkled with pepper.

TWO HOME-MADE SWEETS

The Roman sweets were rather limited, in the absence of sugar and other ingredients which medieval cooks possessed.

| *5 oz dates* | *2 tbs honey* |
| *2 oz pine-kernels* | *sea salt* |

Boil the honey, allow to stand, and skim. Stone the dates and stuff with pine kernels. Salt lightly and fry in the honey for 2–3 minutes. Drain and serve.

| *4 oz hard crust of brown wholemeal* | $\frac{3}{4}$ *pt milk* |
| *bread, broken into large pieces* | *4 oz honey* |

Soak the bread in milk for about an hour. Deep fry in olive oil until well browned and crisp. Drain. Warm honey and pour over before serving.

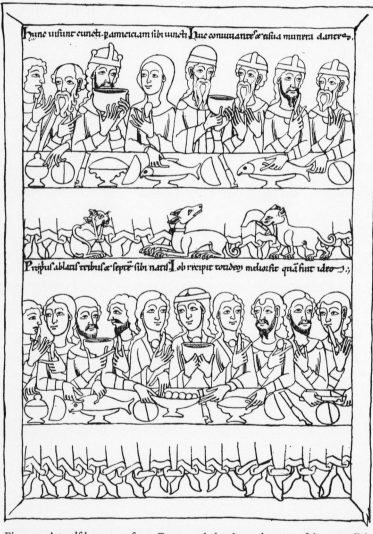

Figure 2 A twelfth-century feast. Everyone helps themselves out of the same dish, using only a knife and a piece of bread (called a trench from the French *tranche* or slice).

The collapse of the Roman Empire and the invasions of the Germanic tribes from the east meant an end of luxury and easy living. The last years of the Empire were marked by a series of edicts designed to control prices and cut down excessive spending, though these failed to check the general economic decay. The decline of the towns and rise of the country villas as the homes of wealthy magnates meant that the social setting in which Roman cookery had flourished no longer existed, and that there was a general return to less exotic ways.

The Germanic peoples themselves had no real contribution to make to the art of cookery. The Romans had enjoyed and sought out the hams and sausages that came from beyond the Rhine, but apart from this the barbarian banquets seem to have harked back to the Homeric feasts: freshly slaughtered and roasted cattle washed down with mead were the basic offering on such occasions. Tacitus speaks of their 'plentiful, if homely fare', while another Roman writer describes them as eating raw meat – though it is possible that he really means smoked or cured meat. One clear indication that cookery was not one of their skills is the way in which the names of foods and other terms used in cookery in modern German are all derived from Latin, while very few other words are borrowed from the Romans. The cook's art was a luxury learnt from their new subjects.

Of the various tribes who occupied the former Roman lands, it was the Franks who adapted most rapidly to the Roman tradition in the kitchen (though it was an Ostrogoth from northern Italy who had his own selection of recipes made from Apicius). Gregory of Tours, writing about the newly converted Franks in the sixth century, complains that one nobleman was such a glutton that he could never be persuaded to observe the Church's fastdays, 'often eating very young rabbits on such days'. Gregory himself describes one dish which he found particularly delicious, 'a hot baking-pan full of the food made from beaten eggs quickly mixed with chopped dates and round olives', and we gather from him that meals still followed the Roman pattern of an *hors d'œuvre*, main courses and sweet.

About the same time we meet the first of the long and distinguished line of French gourmets, Venantius Fortunatus, bishop of Poitiers, '*abbé gastronome*' and poet. Venantius inherited not only the late Latin poetic style, but also some knowledge of Roman cuisine. Here he hails one of his fellow-countrymen, a high-ranking noble, as the new Apicius:

> Nectar and wine and food and scholar's wit
> Such is the fashion, Gogo, of thy house.
> Cicero art thou, and Apicius too,
> But now I cry you mercy: no more goose!
> Where the ox lieth, dare the chickens come?
> Nay, horn and wing unequal warfare keep.
> My eyes are closing and my lute is dumb,
> Slower and slower go my songs to sleep.

On other occasions Venantius commemorates the hospitality of Radégonde, queen and abbess, who sends him mouth-watering dinners, the plates piled high with delicacies. Unfortunately Venantius was a better trencherman than student of cookery, and he does not convey to us what subtleties went into the making of the rather ordinary menu he proceeds to describe: meat with gravy (in silver dishes), chicken, vegetables in a marble dish, and apples. But it must have been tasty, for he confesses rather shamefacedly that he has cheerfully demolished it all himself. Another meal of milk and cream, plums and eggs, makes him exclaim: 'Peace to my stomach after such variety of food!'

Nor did the cooks lack due respect, with such appreciative guests. Gregory of Tours tells how the nephew of the bishop of Langres, captured and enslaved by heathens, was rescued by Leo, the bishop's cook, who arranged for himself to be sold to the same heathen master. When asked what he could do, he replied: 'I am skilled in preparing all the things that ought to be eaten at the tables of masters, and I am not afraid that my equal in skill can be found. For I tell you that even if you desire to make ready a feast for the king, I can prepare kingly viands.' His master replied: '. . . I ask you to make me such a feast as to make my guests wonder and say "We have not seen better in the king's palace."' The banquet he prepared (from 'a great number of cocks and hens') was so excellent that he was put in charge of the household, and was able in due course to escape with the bishop's nephew. But a cook's life was not an easy one: Gregory also tells of a man who started his life as a kitchen slave, but 'as he had weak eyes ill fitted to endure the sharp smoke', he was transferred to the bakery.

Our next glimpse of Frankish eating habits comes from an order circulated to his officers throughout his realms by Charlemagne in the early ninth century, which lays down the rules of good husbandry to be followed on the royal estates. We learn that pastries made with eggs and flour were highly prized, since hens and geese were to be kept and the best flour was to be reserved for their making. A list of prepared items for the storeroom included lard, smoked sausages, ordinary sausages, salt meat, wine, vinegar, mulberry wine, boiled must, garum (i.e. the Roman liquamen), mustard, cheese, butter, malt, beer, mead, honey, wax and flour. Provisions for Lent, now an important factor in eating habits and in the cook's calendar, comprise millet, dried and green herbs and root vegetables. All these were to be in stock against the emperor's arrival at any of his estates, since in an age of difficult transport it was often easier for him to live off the produce on the spot rather than have it taken to a distant city. But the most surprising list is that for the garden, which is a remarkably sophisticated catalogue of plants:

[You are to grow] lilies, roses, fenugreek, costmary, sage, rue, wormwood, cucumbers, peppers, gourds, beans, several types of cumin, rosemary, carraway, pulse, squill, gladioli, snakeweed, aniseed, wild gourds, heliotrope, chervil, lettuces, colewort, cress, mint, alexanders, parsley, lovage, juniper, dill, fennel, endive, dittany, mustard, savory, tansy, catnip, centaury, poppies, beet, hazelwort, hollyhock, mallows, carrots, parsnips, orach, spinach, kohlrabi, cabbage, onions, chives, leeks, radishes, shallotts, garlic, madder, artichokes, broad beans, peas, coriander, spurge and clary. And the gardener is to grow house leeks [*sempervivum*] on his house. As to trees, we wish you to have apple, pear and plum trees of various species, crabapples, medlars, chestnuts, peaches of various kinds, quinces, hazelnut bushes, almond trees, mulberries, laurels, pines, figs, walnuts and cherry trees of various kinds.

The list ends with seven different types of apple tree and five varieties of pear. At first sight, such an array of produce would seem to imply an equally varied output on the cook's part; and certainly many of the ingredients of the most exotic Roman dishes are here. But the herbs were probably grown for their medicinal value, whilst the list itself may have been based on a text-book on agriculture: it is perhaps a civil servant's five-year plan rather than what actually grew in Charlemagne's gardens.

What we know of Charlemagne's table would tend to bear this out. His biographer tells us that:

He was moderate in his eating and drinking, and especially so in drinking; for he hated to see drunkenness in any man, and even more so in himself and his friends. All the same, he could not go long without food, and he often used to complain that fasting made him feel ill. He rarely gave banquets and these only on high feast days, but then he would invite a great number of guests. His main meal of the day was served in four courses, in addition to the roast meat which his hunters used to bring in on spits, and which he enjoyed more than any other food . . . He was so sparing in his use of wine and every other beverage that he rarely drank more than three times in the course of his dinner. In summer, after his midday meal, he would eat some fruit and take another drink.

This fondness for roast meat was frowned upon by his doctors, who advised him unavailingly to eat stewed dishes instead. For cookery was increasingly regarded as a province of medicine. The great Greek physicians, Hippocrates and Galen, had begun to explore the idea that diet had an important effect on health, and in the hands of Arab doctors the theory of 'humours' was worked out in elaborate detail. This idea persisted in cookery to the end of the seventeenth century. Foods were classified as sanguine (moist and hot), choleric (dry and hot), and phlegmatic (moist and cold), melancholic (dry and cold), corresponding to the four elements, air, fire, earth and water respectively. Each individual was believed to have his own predominant humour, and excessive tendencies towards a particular humour, whether as the result of temporary circumstances or illness, or deriving from character, were to be treated by adjusting the patient's diet.

Medical lore also gives us the few glimpses we have of Anglo-Saxon cookery. Among the 'leechdoms, wortcraft and star-cunning' (medical, herbal and astronomical lore) of the period, a small number of references to food are to be found. Beef, veal, mutton, pork, goat and venison, poultry and wildfowl of various kinds, and native fish and shellfish all appeared on the table; bees were kept for their all-important honey; fruit was cultivated, but vegetables such as lettuce, radishes and cabbage were gathered in their wild form as worts. The treatment of these viands, however, was fairly elementary, consisting of pies, or, in the case of poultry, stuffings. Otherwise we learn only of invalid foods, such as milk preparations or junkets, of the kind one would expect in a medical book. Spices were certainly imported, and the mention of pepper and cumin seeds shows how widespread the network of trade remained, even if only small quantities were involved. We hear of St Boniface on his missions to the Germans in the eighth century being sent cinnamon, pepper and other spices from Rome, though these could also have been used in medicines.

In the eighth century, under the relative peace and prosperity of Charlemagne's rule, copies of Apicius's book were made in south Germany and at Tours in France, but no great revival of classical cookery appears in the following centuries. The records are admittedly very sparse, but what we find in the thirteenth century shows very little change from the Frankish or Anglo-Saxon diet of five centuries earlier. Just as the abbess Radégonde had earned poetic fame for her cooking, so it is in the monasteries and cathedrals that good living becomes a tradition in the later Middle Ages. The table of the canons of Basle about 1180–90 included, on fish days, such items as salmon cooked in oil with leeks, trout in vinegar, pike in pepper sauce, cod with mustard, and a kind of whitebait. At festivals when meat could be eaten, the offerings comprised hams, three types of sausage, *charcuterie* of various sorts, smoked beef on cabbage, grilled and roast pork, roast boar garnished with venison, and a dish of millet mixed with eggs, milk and pigs' blood. St Anselm too would seem to have had a monk in mind when in his work on morals he deals with the pleasures of the senses. Distinguishing, in the best medieval philosophical style between five simple, ten double, ten triple and five quadruple pleasures, he chooses as an example for the double pleasure of taste and smell 'when someone eats immoderate quantities of chicken spiced with pepper and cumin'. Perhaps, since these two spices are specifically mentioned in Anglo-Saxon records (and Anselm was archbishop of Canterbury), this was a native delicacy.

But luxury on a Roman scale was still unheard of; only the gorgeous and outrageous East could trade in splendours to really horrify a worthy western cleric. Here is another eleventh-century writer, Peter Damian, inveighing against the Byzantines:

The Doge of Venice had married a lady from Constantinople, whose luxury surpassed all imagination. She would not even wash in common water, but had the cruelty to compel her servants to collect rain water for her . . . But what is monstrous, this wicked creature would not eat with her fingers, but absolutely had her food cut into pieces, minutely, by her attendants, and then conveyed them to her mouth with certain golden two-pronged forks.

For the common fork was unknown in the West, and was not to come into general use until the seventeenth century, a factor which profoundly affected the way in which medieval food was cooked. With only a pointed knife, a spoon and a breadsop as implements, it was difficult to cut food on the plate, and dishes consisting of meat in an elaborate sauce had to be reduced to a consistency which could be managed with a spoon. Hence a meal would consist of roast meat or pâtés and purées of various kinds.

In general, medieval cooking equipment was rather simpler than that of the Romans, and few houses had their own ovens. Baking was a professional skill, like milling. At home, the cooking cauldron – now made of metal instead of earthenware – was the chief utensil, with a meat hook for removing the contents from the boiling water. Frying pans were found only in large houses, and were little different from the Roman pattern, and a crude form of charcoal grill was occasionally used. The pestle and mortar were as important as ever.

Much of the cook's time was taken up with buying and preserving foodstuffs, and it was impossible to keep large stocks of food which was ready to eat. So in the large towns the cookshop, an institution which the Romans had known, reappeared. Here is a description of one in twelfth-century London, where the difficulty of obtaining supplies from the surrounding countryside was becoming a problem:

Moreover there is in London upon the river's bank, amid the wine that is sold from ships and wine-cellars, a public cook-shop. There daily, according to the season, you may find viands, dishes roast, fried and boiled, fish great and small, the coarser flesh for the poor, the more delicate for the rich, such as venison and birds both big and little. If friends, weary with travel, should of a sudden come to any of the citizens and it is not their pleasure to wait until fresh food is bought and cooked and 'until servants bring water for hands and bread,' they hasten to the river bank, and there all things desirable are ready to their hand. However great the infinitude of knights or foreigners that enter the city or are about to leave it, at whatever hour of the night or day, that the former may not fast too long nor the latter depart without their dinner they turn aside thither, if it so please them, and refresh themselves each after his own manner. Those who desire to fare delicately need not search to find sturgeon or 'guinea-fowl' or 'Ionian francolin', since all the dainties that are found there are set forth before their eyes. Now this is a public cookshop, appropriate to a city and pertaining to the art of civic life.

The cook's secrets, like those of the masons, were handed down by word of mouth; we do not possess any twelfth- or thirteenth-century recipes. On the other hand, we do know something about the food and feasts of the period. King John's household accounts at the beginning of the thirteenth century show that he bought enormous quantities of food for his Christmas feast, but that the fare was not particularly spectacular: pork, chicken, a small number of pheasants and other game, much fish, salt eels and herrings, and a selection of spices – pepper, cloves, cinnamon, nutmegs, ginger and saffron for colouring. A hundred pounds of almonds went into the sauces. Although the range of herbs and spices was nothing like as wide as the Roman, it was a considerable advance on what would have been used a hundred years earlier. The bishop of Hereford's Christmas spice cupboard in 1289 was replenished with a much wider variety again: cloves, cubebs, mace, saffron, galingale, cinnamon, ginger, pepper, cumin, liquorice, aniseed, coriander and gromwell. The meat for his feast consisted of ten oxen, eight pigs, sixty chickens, one boar and three calves. About the same time, a kind of ideal menu for such an occasion was described by Walter de Bibbesworth:

A servant came here lately from a feast, and told us how the serving of the meal was arranged. Without bread and wine and beer a feast would be a poor affair, but the feasters had all three, and well chosen too. To start with, a boar's head all arrayed with banners of flowers on its snout was brought in: then venison and frumenty, as much as was needed in the house at such a time. Then there were various roasts for everyone, cranes, peacocks, swans, wild geese, kids, pigs and hens. The third course was rabbits in gravy, and meat cooked in Cyprus wine, with mace, cubebs and cloves, washed down with quantities of red and white wine. Then there were pheasants, woodcock and partridges, fieldfares, larks and plovers all well roasted, and brawn and crêpes and fried things, all sprinkled with rose sugar. After the meal there were plenty of blaunche poudre [? sweets made with icing sugar] and big dragées.

This is obviously an imaginary occasion, and indeed the menu was copied in several romances of chivalry down to the fifteenth century, when we find King Arthur giving it to the Roman ambassadors.

Both in the bishop's list of spices and in Walter de Bibbesworth's feast an important new ingredient appears: sugar. The bishop's agent bought three baskets, weighing fifty-four pounds, of this exotic luxury, and this is the first mention of it in English. It was largely used to decorate dishes in powder form, and honey remained the main sweetening agent for some time. The Crusaders had been the first Europeans to see sugar-cane, as they marched towards Tripoli in the Lebanon in 1099, and it was from the Frankish kingdom of Palestine that most of western Europe's supply came until 1300, when the Arabs overran the Christian territories.

Other items among the bishop's spices came from even more distant lands, for the spice trade, which had continued on a small scale since Roman times, now flourished once again. The Crusades had led to a ban by the Pope on trading with the Arabs, but nevertheless the Italians established a regular commerce with them. The Arabs in turn obtained cinnamon from the East Indies; cubebs (a kind of black pepper), nutmeg and mace, made from the nutmeg husk, also came from there, brought either overland or in dhows round the coast to the Persian Gulf. All these were novelties in England, though the Anglo-Saxons had used cassia, a spice related to cinnamon, in medicine. Ginger, also for medicinal use, had continued to reach Europe in small quantities since Roman times, but was now brought from the Far East in considerable shipments. Aniseed, cumin and coriander were obtainable in the Mediterranean, while the saffron crocus, gromwell and liquorice root were native plants.

All this points to some knowledge of how to concoct complex spiced dishes; but we have no definite evidence of what the results were like until we turn to thirteenth-century Italy. And here we meet our first real gourmets since Apicius and his friends. In about 1285 a group of twelve young noblemen of Siena, lovers of good living and high spending, decided to pool all their resources and to lead as luxurious an existence as possible until their combined wealth was exhausted. Among their number was one Niccolò de' Salimbeni, who, as Dante tells us,

> . . . first found out
> How to make cloves a costly cult and passion
> In the garden where such seeds take root and sprout.

Early commentators on Dante's poem suggested a number of explanations for this remark. One writer, confusing the imagery of the next line with the cult of cloves – Dante means that he sowed the use of such extravagances among his fellow-spendthrifts – explained that Niccolò used to grow cloves and basil in the same piece of ground because this gave a better flavour to the cloves; others say that he was the first to roast pheasants and partridges with cloves, or simply the first to introduce cloves to Siena (though this seems unlikely, as they were already known as far afield as England). A more thoughtful commentator offers various opinions:

Some say that this Niccolò made his servants clean [grate ?] cloves for him, but this is easier said than done. Others say that he put cloves into roast meats, but this was neither a new invention nor any great extravagance. Others say that he had pheasants and chickens roasted over a fire made of cloves. And this I do believe, because it was the vainest and most extravagant habit, an entirely new invention; and there are similar stories about him to the effect that he had gold florins cooked in sauce, which he would suck and throw away.

But the most interesting detail comes from Francesco da Buti, writing in about 1380:

This Niccolò de' Salimbeni was one of the Spendthrift Brigade, and because they all tried to discover sumptuous and gluttonous dishes, it is said that blancmanges and Ubaldine fritters were invented then, and other similar things, about which their cook wrote a book.

It is this book, which survives in a fragment known simply as *A Book of Cookery*, that is our earliest surviving practical medieval cookery book. There are Latin collections of recipes, but as we shall see these are more for medicinal purposes than for use in the kitchen, even though they are older. One indication that *A Book of Cookery* is indeed the work written for the Spendthrift Brigade is the number of recipes in it for twelve people; another is the striking number of exotic elements. And, even more interesting, we can trace the pedigree of many of the recipes. Just as Arab learning had become the basis of western medicine and science, so these novel ideas are drawn from Arab sources, by way of Sicily.

The first direct translation of an Arab cookery book of which we know is only a little earlier than the Spendthrift Brigade; it is the *Book of Dishes and Spices*, by Ibn Gazla of Baghdad, and the translator, the delightfully named Jambobinus of Cremona, may have studied at the medical school at Salerno. It was at Salerno that Arab theories on medicine were largely introduced to the West, and after the accession of the Angevins (with their French connections) in 1284, these ideas became more widely known in the West. The French were already reputed to be much addicted to easy living, and had disgraced themselves on several occasions during the Crusades by an excessive fondness for eastern ways. But they had brought back little from their exploration of eastern food; only when they encountered these already partly Europeanized recipes did they really take to the use of exotic dishes as a regular feature of their cooking.

The kind of material in question can be found in Arnold de Villanova's book, *Rules for Health*, written about 1300. Villanova devotes a chapter to the use of spices, and although he is more concerned with the effects of spices on the constitution, he gives an interesting picture of the new resources available to a cook. Lard, oil and butter – the latter a novelty since Roman days, adopted from Germanic tradition – were the principal fats, while oils included olive oil, nut oil, flax oil, poppyseed oil 'which some people use' and almond oil. Salt, as one would expect, is the principal seasoning.

Villanova's approach is best summed up by his remark that it is not a good idea to use too appetizing a seasoning, as this makes men eat more than is good for them. In particular – and here we come back to the idea of the four humours mentioned earlier – the less a sauce resembles a food which it accompanies, the less of it should be used to achieve a balance: so vegetables, which are earthy and melancholic, should be cooked in a very small amount of butter, which is airy and sanguine. Hot sauces should be avoided in summer. Elaborate sauces are on the whole the invention of gluttons bent on the pleasures of the senses rather than on improving their health, says Villanova, and hence have no place in a medical work. He does, however, give a green sauce for chicken which seems quite elaborate: in summer, it should be made of 'vinegar and verjuice* and a very few spices', i.e. with garlic, parsley, a little white ginger and a little toasted bread soaked in vinegar or verjuice. In winter the same sauce should be made with more spice and a little garlic, best wine and a little verjuice; otherwise mustard and colewort would be enough. Apart from the ginger it is not so far off the sauce which James II recommended to Samuel Pepys almost four hundred years later:

Here he dined, and did mightily magnify his sauce, which he did then eat with everything, and said it was the best universal sauce in the world, it being taught him by the Spanish ambassador; made of some parsley and a dry toast, beat in a mortar, together with vinegar, salt and a little pepper; he eats it with flesh or fowl, or fish: . . . and by and by did taste it, and liked it mightily.

As to meats, Villanova recommends a gravy for beef made of the juices of the meat, pepper, toast and a little verjuice, while cold pork is offered as an *hors d'œuvre* with vinegar and parsley.

These brief indications were elaborated by Maino Mainerio some forty years later into a kind of book of sauces. The result is almost a brief survey of cookery, as he offers various ways of treating the main ingredients. Here are his instructions for chicken:

* This was unsweetened grape or apple juice. Modern grape juice tends to be too sweet, and apple juice is a better substitute.

The sauce for boiled chickens and pheasants is their stock with pounded sweet spices added to it: in particular in winter hyssop, sage and parsley are to be added, in summer enough stock with green sorrel juice or vine tips. Or a white sauce can be made, with almonds instead of walnuts and white sugar added. If they are cooked whole in pastry, cook with verjuice and pounded spices in summer; in winter, add a little good wine. If they are cut up and cooked in pastry, add lard and sage and hyssop and parsley with sweet strong spices. If they are roasted, use garlic sauce with almonds . . . or sweet wine beaten with almonds in winter, and a little spice and verjuice in summer.

The white sauce to which he refers is given earlier in the work for use with meat, and is one of the few medieval recipes to give quantities, though weights and measures of the period varied so much from place to place that one cannot be certain that modern equivalents are the same: 1 lb sweet almonds, 1 oz ground ginger, ½ qt verjuice; temper with meat stock. A gravy for veal is more detailed, and also gives precise quantities:

Take toasted brown bread soaked in vinegar, an ounce of ground pepper, 1 lb melted lard in which the meat has been fried, 15 shallots. Fry the onions and make the gravy with meat stock, the bread and the best onions pounded in a mortar with the pepper. Boil all together until thick.

Our modern word 'recipe' comes from these Latin instructions which begin 'Take . . .', in Latin '*Recipe* . . .'

One entirely modern sauce which Mainerio gives is that for roast pork, consisting simply of the gravy from the meat with wine and onions; pigeons and partridges require no seasoning except perhaps lemon juice, and in general he is fairly conservative in his use of spices. In addition to those already mentioned, he employs rosemary, cinnamon, grains of paradise and cloves, with saffron for colouring. For fish, he tends to prefer hot sauces, in which pepper, ginger and cloves predominate, though the green sauce used with chicken is also recommended for crab. In a less appetizing vein, he offers a method of preserving porpoise for up to ten days by jellying it.

The basis of the cookery book of the Spendthrift Brigade was a Latin work written in Angevin circles in southern Italy, drawing on the same material as the two books we have just looked at. This they translated, adding a number of their own recipes; and the version that we have includes a few more homely items which were probably added later. For three recipes whose titles betray their Arab origin, we have exact equivalents from Arab sources, and it is interesting to set them side by side. Here are the two versions of *sommachia* as given in the originals:

ITALIAN: Take dismembered chickens, fry in lard. Take almonds, sumac, and water, and cook with chicken. Make sure it is well thickened.

ARAB: Slice fat meat, put in pot, and season with spiced salt. Boil until almost completely cooked. Skim well. Add beet cut to finger-thick pieces and carrots. Take onions and leeks, peel, wash in salt water and add. If aubergines are available, skin and add, after part-cooking separately. Take sumac, put in separate pan, add salt and breadcrumbs, cook well and strain. Add jointed chicken. Chop red meat and make small spiced meatballs: add these. Add spices: green coriander, cumin, pepper, ginger, cinnamon, mastic, chopped finely with bouquets of fresh mint. Take the prepared sumac and add. Chop walnuts, moisten, and add. Crumble in dried mint and unchopped walnuts. Chop a little garlic, boil in water and add. Some add eggs on serving. Simmer until reduced.

Modern versions of the two recipes for *limonia* are given on pp. 66–7. The pair of recipes for *romania* run as follows in the originals:

ITALIAN: Fry chickens in lard and onions. Grind almonds with the skin on, and dilute in juice of sweet or bitter pomegranates. Squeeze well, strain and add liquid to chickens. Boil, mix with a spoon or beat. Add spices. If pomegranates are not available, make a sauce with herbs.

ARAB: Cut up fat meat into strips of medium size and put in pot with spiced salt. Cover with water, boil and skim. Peel aubergines and quarter them. Peel and slice onions. Clean gourds, remove seeds and pulp and cut into strips. Parboil separately, then add to pot. Add coriander, cumin, cinnamon, pepper and bunches of mint and cook well. Finally take sour pomegranates, shell by hand, squeeze and strain. Add to pot. Shred dried mint and put on top. Add peeled garlic. Chicken in pieces may be added to cook with the meat. Simmer for an hour.

The gourds mentioned are similar to courgettes (which came

originally from America) and the latter would be a suitable substitute.

The complexity of Arab cookery was partly due to a longer tradition of written cookery books. The earliest recorded work of this kind in Arabic dates from the middle of the tenth century, and in 1239 the author of a treatise on cookery – at a time when they were virtually unknown in Europe – could say that he had consulted a large number of them in the course of his work; the names, though not the works, of ten cookery writers of the tenth century have come down to us, all of them connected with the luxury-loving court of the Abbassid dynasty at Baghdad, including the notable doctor Ibn Mazawiah, and even the general postmaster Ibn Khordadhbeh; some of these lengthy tomes were in verse, as befitted an art 'of which no cultured man should be ignorant'. Elaborate ceremonies made dining into a daily ritual; and meals became immensely costly and varied, a far cry from the 'despised foods' of the early Muslims, rice and dates with cream and honey (*kabissa*) or flour, butter and honey (*faludadsch*). Instead, a man was reckoned miserly if he had only ten dishes at his midday meal; display was all, for one caliph economized in 937 by cutting down the sweets served each day from thirty to 'as many as he needed'; and for the first time we meet delicacies made of sugar for show, castles, buildings and figures. This tradition was continued by the Fatimid caliphs of Egypt in the eleventh century; a Persian traveller described in 1040 how nearly 200,000 pounds of sugar were used for the sultan's table at the feast at the end of Ramadan, the month of fasting: 'On the table stood a lemon tree whose twigs, fruits and leaves were all of sugar, and a thousand statues and figures as well.'

Nonetheless, all this luxury concealed a simple traditional approach to preparing food. For instance, in an elaborate thirteenth-century cookery book, the basic fat is still mutton fat taken from the sheep's tail, and two famous peasant dishes are included, handed down from the days when the Arabs had been nomads. Beef never appeared; the pork beloved of the Romans was of course an 'unclean meat' to the Muslim; and mutton reigned supreme. A very wide range of fruits was used, and the recipes came from a wide area. Basically much of the cookery is Persian.

The Persians were renowned as inventors of luxurious dishes long before the court at Baghdad reached its zenith, and it is a curious thought that many of our ideas about *haute cuisine* may derive from the dishes prepared by Belshazzar's cooks for his feast. On the one hand, we have already seen that much of Greek and Roman cookery derived from the Middle East, while we now find thirteenth-century Europe returning indirectly to the same source by way of Arab cookery. The Arabs, however, were prepared to range further afield in search of new delicacies, and dishes from Georgia, Byzantium, North Africa, Egypt and South Arabia all figured in the Baghdad menus. A particular feature of the luxurious cooking of this period was attention to small details – which becomes a kind of fastidiousness for its own sake – and search for pungent flavours, as in Roman days. At the other extreme, here is one which can only be regarded as a curiosity, and must have been dreamt up as a novelty for a bored gourmet with indigestion who had been forbidden his usual rich diet:

Bottled omelette: mix omelette, put in tightly stoppered bottle. Boil until cooked. Break the glass carefully, and the omelette will retain the shape of the bottle.

Another recipe is for mock brains, to be made of liver, which seems a somewhat pointless exercise for the period, though it might have its uses today, when only the standard and generally accepted cuts of meat are on sale.

It is hardly surprising that the innovators of the Spendthrift Brigade found Arab cookery to their liking. But the cook who compiled the recipes they had used included a number of less elaborate items, perhaps for the benefit of his fellow craftsmen whose patrons might not have such eccentric tastes, both from Arab and Italian sources. *Brodo sarta cenito* or Saracen stew is one example of a fairly simple dish of Arab origin, while other dishes bear familiar geographical names such as 'chicken provençale' and 'chicken espagnole', though the results are somewhat different from the modern meanings. Chicken provençale, or *brodo dei capponi a la provenzale*, turns out as a kind of chicken omelette (p. 70), while chicken espagnole can be made with not only chicken but any other kind of meat. Much space is given to vegetables, though the directions are usually limited to saying which spices should be used with each of them. Occasionally a more elaborate dish results, as with the two recipes for onions and peas (*piselli con carne*) on p. 70. Pasta, in the form of *ravioli*, makes its first appearance, and 'Ubaldo's fritters', which the commentator of Dante singled out as one of the Sienese inventions, are also given (p. 74). Other sweet dishes include nougat and junket; the former includes a direction which points to fairly primitive conditions in the kitchen, since the cook is directed to wet the palm of his hand with water and spread the nougat mixture on it until it cools – perhaps to be 'handed out' without more ado.

If *A Book of Cookery* is a very important milestone in the history of cookery, the nearest there is to a medieval equivalent of Apicius, later cooks naturally collected recipes from elsewhere. Although it is often very difficult to tell where a dish might have come from, different nations were beginning to acquire a reputation for eating particular kinds of food, as Enrique de Villena points out in the introduction to his Spanish cookery book in 1384. Already there is a suitable disdain for the odd ways of foreigners: according to him, the Turks eat horses, the French and Italians snakes, the inhabitants of Andalusia grasshoppers, and the Catalans gnaw bones. On the other hand, there is no such easy guidance when we want to trace the origin of a well-known medieval dish such as *blanc manger* (not to be confused under any circumstances with blancmange). It could be Spanish: Robert de Nola, writing in the fifteenth century, calls it one of the three best sauces in the world, 'each of which deserves its own royal crown', the others being *pavon* and *mirauste*; and chicken, the main ingredient of *blanc manger*, is a staple of early Spanish cookery. There is too a Spanish proverb of the period, that 'peasants don't eat *manjar bianco*' (the Spanish name for *blanc manger*). But on the other hand it appears in *A Book of Cookery*, and we shall meet it again in English cookery books; it is from the latter that the recipe on p.74 is taken. Its most likely source is once again Arabic cookery which was well known to both Spaniards and Italians.

The small store of recipes in *A Book of Cookery* was soon increased by new contributions, notably from the French. Many of the apparently new items may simply be traditional dishes which are now recorded for the first time, since our evidence for twelfth- and early thirteenth-century cookery is so slight that we can only guess at the recipes used. The first French work on cookery is a small treatise which appears at the end of a manuscript containing a Latin version of *A Book of Cookery*, dating from about 1300. It contains forty-four entries on the preparation of meat and fish, 'which anyone who wishes to serve in a great establishment should have written on his heart; whoever does not will never please his master'. The writer emphasizes that these are ways of cooking drawn from 'different traditions and different countries', though some are merely a note of the appropriate condiment, for example: 'Fresh salmon, with hot pepper; salted, with mustard, in summer and winter'.

Pork was the basic meat in the medieval diet, chiefly because it could be obtained fresh all the year round, and also because it was the best of the salted meats in winter. It therefore received more elaborate treatment, as in the pork stew on p. 69. Other meats were to be roasted or boiled, though veal pasties are mentioned. The greatest delicacy was sucking pig, which is prepared with hard-boiled eggs, chestnuts, cheese and a particular kind of pear. Chickens, geese and wildfowl appear – the poultry cooked in garlic, already a favourite French seasoning – as well as the swans and peacocks which were the showpieces on a medieval dining table. Curiously, the lord was to be given 'the neck and the head, the wings and the thighs' of these birds as his particular portion, while we would regard the breast as the tenderest meat. Other meats used for pasties are goat and rabbit.

The first section on meat in its simple form is followed by more varied recipes based on chicken – 'blanc douchet', 'cominée', 'blanc brouet' and others, among them a 'subtle English stew' which uses an interesting sauce (see p. 71). There is also a 'Saracen stew', but it is very different from that in *A Book of Cookery*; instead of chicken cooked with fruit, it is composed of eels in cinnamon, cloves and (apparently) lavender. Almost as unusual in a different way is 'cominée' of fish, which instead of the outlandish mixture of spices of the preceding recipe, uses one spice only, cumin pounded with almonds, with which the fish is stuffed. Almonds also appear in other sauce recipes; since white flour was very expensive and the medieval kitchen had no white roux, they remained the basic body for sauces until the seventeenth century. In pounded form, they were conveniently moist, and also offered a smoother consistency than the rough wholemeal flour of the period. (White bread was a great luxury, due to the cost of white flour, and is specified only in the most lavish recipes, as *paindemain*.) Almond milk, a blend of pounded almonds and milk, is another stock ingredient where a more fluid consistency is required; it forms the basis of the kind of rice pudding which replaced *blanc manger* in Lent, when no meat was allowed (p. 74). As to fish, the instructions for this are mostly recommendations for spices: roast mackerel are to be eaten with 'cameline sauce', made of cinnamon and ginger moistened with vinegar – but no garlic, the author insists. Pike is one of the most frequently used fishes, and there is a recipe for oyster stew; but carp, with which any good fishpond of the next century would be stocked, were not yet known in France.

The first medieval cookery book writer whose name has come down to us is Guillaume Tirel, lord of Taillevent, whose career can be traced from 1326 to his death in 1395. Such a long lifespan is unusual in an age when a man was old at forty, and it has been argued that the records must refer to a man and his son; yet if he entered the royal service as a young boy, he might still have been under eighty when he died. His progress in the royal household as shown in the records supports the latter idea, for he rose steadily in rank, becoming cook to Philip of Valois and then to Charles V, and ending as master of the kitchens to Charles VI. His fine tombstone at St-Germain-en-Laye depicted him as a person of some importance, in full knightly panoply, with his two wives on either side of him.

His book, called the *Viandier de Guillaume Taillevent* (Guillaume Taillevent's Book of Food) was, as far as we can tell, the work of his latter years, being completed about 1380. It is not a particularly original compilation, and much of the material is taken from the two books we have already discussed. But it became the basis for a number of later works, and in particular was one of the first French cookery books to be printed, in 1492, so that it influenced much of French sixteenth-century cooking. Recipes from

Figure 3 Memorial brass of Guillaume Taillevent, cook to the kings of France.

it are given on pp. 71 and 68; among them is one which is the first mention of an *haricot*, a word whose origin is obscure, while a recipe for peas is not unlike that given in Apicius. In the latter, the dish is named after a vegetable rather than the meat used, in contrast to usual modern practice.

Taillevent has curiously few 'show' recipes, and his book is not very different from one compiled for a rather humbler household in Paris not long afterwards. *Le Menagier de Paris* (*The Parisian Housekeeper* is a kind of very early Mrs Beeton, and much of the book is concerned with the management of a citizen's establishment, say a rich merchant's house. A large section of it is devoted to cookery, and it may be that the writer used Taillevent's own book as well as a manuscript containing another collection called *The Most Excellent Book of Cookery* which is known only from a printed version of 1542. *The Parisian Housekeeper* reflects many of the problems which faced the cook. There is lengthy advice on how to buy meat, fish and vegetables, where and when the best markets in Paris are held, how to tell fresh provisions from old or stale supplies, and when the best season for any commodity may be. Meat in particular was a problem. There was of course no refrigeration of any kind, and about this time the difficulties of supplying a town were just becoming apparent. Paris was probably the largest city in western Europe, and was steadily growing in size. The population was now so considerable that the countryside immediately around the city could no longer support the townsfolk, and food had to be transported from some distance away in carts that could move at little more than walking pace over the rudimentary tracks which passed for roads. As early as the twelfth century decrees on the management of the food markets were common, part of the usual business of the city elders. Much of this legislation was aimed at controlling prices, since the organization of the various trades into closely-knit guilds meant that there was a series of virtual monopolies in different products. Furthermore, trades became family specialities, and even at the end of the nineteenth century in Limoges, the butcher's trade was concentrated in two medieval streets and in the hands of three or four families. Equally important was the problem of buying in provisions, because in order to prevent hoarding and artificial

1 to 4. A famous sequence of miniatures from the Luttrell Psalter showing the preparation and serving of a meal in the fourteenth century. From the top, they show roasting of chickens and sucking pig at an open fire (notice how large a blaze is needed); stewing in cooking pots, beating meat, and pounding in a large pestle and mortar; cutting up meat and serving it; and the company at table.

5. William I feasting before the battle of Hastings, from the Bayeux tapestry. The inscription reads: 'Here the meat is cooked, and here the servers served it; here the feast was made, and here the bishop blessed the food and drink.'

6. A feast from a medieval German manuscript of the tenth century.

scarcities, food vendors were not allowed to keep large stocks or to sell to other dealers or middlemen. To buy food in one market with the intention of reselling it at a higher price in another was an offence, known by the name of 'regrating'; but it was far from uncommon, as streetnames such as the Rue de la Regratterie in Poitiers show. In general, however, meat and fish would be bought by the housekeeper when they were at their cheapest, and salted down; fruit – which was often regarded as dangerous to health when fresh – would be made into preserves, and all the small preparations which we now buy ready-made would also be manufactured within the household.

The section on cooking in *The Parisian Housekeeper* begins with a series of hints on cookery which must have been part of a medieval cook's basic knowledge. 'When making a sauce with spices and bread, pound the spices first and then the bread, since the bread will take up any spices remaining in the mortar, and nothing will be lost.' There is a notable reversal of modern ideas in a remark about sauces and soups: the sauces are to be strained to make them clear, while the spices and bindings put into soups are to be left as they are in order to thicken it as much as possible. Soups – or rather various kinds of stew – figure largely in the book, and there are instructions on how to avoid burning them, a distinct problem when cooking was done over an almost unregulated heat. There are also hints on how to repair the damage once disaster had befallen the soup. And there are instructions in technical terms: note the difference, the writer says, between *boutonner,* to stick with cloves, and *larder,* to lard with strips of fat, when preparing meat.

For the first time there is a series of menus for different occasions, fifteen in all, for dinners of four to six courses with up to thirty-one dishes. The compiling of menus was a much more serious problem when seasonal availability controlled the possible combinations, and by the seventeenth century it had become such an art that some books dealt with little else, leaving the preparation entirely to the cook's own skill. Here is a fairly simple meal in two courses:

First course: White leeks, beef, goose and chine of pork pasties, jugged hare and rabbits, a dish made with aloes, fat meat.

Second course: Roast boar's tail with piquant sauce, *blanc manger*, potted goose, 'larded milk with crusts' (perhaps a kind of junket), venison, gilded pastry, jellies, milk crusts with egg and almond sauce, chicken pies, cold sage pudding, beef and brains.

Many of the everyday recipes are designed for economy. *Gramose* is made of the left-overs of a joint, and is a common type of medieval dish, consisting of slices of already cooked meat in a sauce (p. 72). 'Soup for when you are taken unawares', or perhaps just 'unready soup', is a standby for sudden emergencies, though a hungry traveller would find it rather thin fare. The section on thick soups, or rather stews, begins with another general instruction to the cook:

First of all, note that all spices which are to be put into a soup must be well pounded and not sieved, except for jelly; and in all soups one should use the sharpest spices one has, because the sooner they are put into a dish the more they lose their flavour; and one should sift pounded bread.

Bread or breadcrumbs are used in a variety of ways, whether for browning, binding or cleaning spices from the mortar, or in a typical soup like *gravé* or *semée*, to be eaten in winter (p. 68). Another emergency recipe is called 'cover-up meat' (*houssebarre de char*) and 'is made quickly for supper when people come unexpectedly' (p. 72).

For grander occasions, there is the menu for a wedding dinner. 'as given by master Helye on a Tuesday in May'. The day and month are important, as Friday was a fish day, and the month would of course indicate what produce was available. The author notes that there were no cherries to be had, and gives the following menu:

Soups: chickens as in *blanc manger*, with pomegranate, and red sugar on top [an echo of the Italian *romania*?]
Roast: a quarter of a kid in each dish – 'a quarter of a kid is better than a lamb' – a gosling, two chickens; sauces: oranges, cinnamon and verjuice.
Entremets: crayfish, loach, rabbit and pork in jelly
Dessert: frumenty and venison
End course: hippocras and accompaniments
Afterwards: wine and spices.

A suitable dish for such an occasion is among a group of recipes passed on by Hotin, cook to M. de Roubaix, 'which he sent in writing', and which appear at the end of the main compilation; it is for chicken with oranges, oranges still being a novelty (p. 69). It is a variation on 'gallimaufry or lazy sauce', also for chicken, which consisted of mustard, ginger, vinegar, stock and verjuice. Oranges were first introduced into France about a century before *The Parisian Housekeeper* was written; the earliest mention of them is in 1333, but since Queen Eleanor was able to buy them from a ship in Southampton in 1290, it seems likely that they were occasionally available in France well before the 1330s. Other items familiar today appear here for the first time, among them a kind of smoked salmon ('baconnée'), and the earliest omelettes, for which the cook is instructed to take seven eggs less two whites.

The Parisian Housekeeper gives a remarkably full picture of fourteenth-century cooking; where other books are almost clinical in their approach, this author gives us the little details which make the cook's methods come to life, as well as hints and ideas gathered from other cooks. On the other hand, there is nothing in it about the range of the equipment available in a fourteenth-century kitchen. All we have to go on for this are the rather dry lists given in accounts and inventories, like that of the kitchen utensils in the household of the queen dowager, Jeanne d'Evreux, when she died in 1328:

2 large sauce pans	4 iron pans in bad condition
16 casseroles	3 brass tongs
3 frying pans	2 iron pans
4 gridirons	2 large cauldrons
8 spit supports	4 other little cauldrons
3 brass sieves	12 assorted large and medium
2 iron sieves	cauldrons
1 *musel de buef* (perhaps an iron	15 little cauldrons
framework for enclosing a joint	1 iron fire-rake
on the spit)	2 dripping pans
1 copper mortar with iron pestle	1 iron tripod
1 skimming spoon	1 barrel
1 copper pot	

The abundance of cauldrons shows how much food was boiled, and this included much of the meat. Roasting was an extravagant process, in terms of both fuel and time, and a spitjack had to turn the joint, basting it almost continually if the meat was not to be dried up. As a protection against the heat, old archery-targets of straw, soaked in water, were used, much as a lady in the Georgian era would have had a little circular fire-screen to protect her. Ovens were used only by bakers, as the absence of any oven trays or other equipment shows; pies would probably have been sent out for baking, except in the very largest households with their own bakery. A surprising omission is the essential meat hook, used for retrieving joints from the cauldrons, though the skimming spoon for the fat is there. The mortar was still an important weapon in the cook's armoury, and like the spices pounded in it, an expensive item.

Even so, the medieval cook was quite capable of composing an elaborate recipe on occasions. Here is one from a long poem on hunting by Gaces de la Bigne, chaplain to three kings of France in the fourteenth century. The original is in verse, but even in plain prose it is complex enough, forerunner of the seventeenth-century extravaganzas of the pie-maker's art:

Put for me in the middle of the pasty three large, well-fed partridges; take care not to leave out six big quails to go by their side. Then take for me a dozen larks and arrange them round the quails, and then thrushes and other little birds, according to what you can get, to garnish the pasty. Then you must provide a little bacon, not at all rancid, dice it and sprinkle it into the pasty. If you want it to be a good one, add verjuice and sprinkle a very little salt on it. Put eggs into it, and make the crust of pure wheat flour . . . Do not put in spices or cheese . . . Put it into a well-heated oven which is clean of ashes, and when it is cooked it will be an excellent dish.

The instructions to leave out spices and cheese sound like the personal preference of someone who has suffered from enthusiastic cooks emptying the spice cupboard into dishes; it is rare to meet a medieval recipe where the variety of spices does not match the variety of other ingredients!

There is one famous vision of a gourmet's heaven from this period which has become a byword. This is the Land of Cockaigne, which appears in satirical poetry of the fourteenth century directed against the luxurious ways of monks. Cockaigne is perhaps a corruption of the Latin *coquina*, a kitchen; there are versions of the poem in French, English, Spanish and Italian. Here is the description of the abbey in Cockaigne from the English poem:

> All of pasties be the walls
> Of flesh, of fish and rich meat
> The tastiest that man may eat
> Wheat flour cakes be all the tiles
> Of church and cloister, bower and hall
> The rooftops are fat puddings
> Rich food for princes and kings.

In the middle of the cloister a tree has roots of ginger, boughs of sandalwood, flowers of mace, bark of cinnamon and cloves as fruit. From the countryside around, the geese roast themselves and fly to the abbey, calling 'Geese all hot, all hot', and bringing their own garlic sauce with them. The French poem adds a few other details: anyone who sleeps till midday is paid $5\frac{1}{2}$ sous, while there are tables laid in every street. Three times a week it rains 'a deluge of hot tarts', while the buildings are made up of fish, bass, salmon and shad, with roofs of bacon and sausages. This combination of a hungry poet's dream and a sluggard's paradise echoed down the centuries in painting and literature. Brueghel's picture embroiders the story with a few new details, while it underlines the unspoken thought behind the dream, the fear of poverty and want which was an ever-present threat. (Plate 9)

Another allegorical poem describes the battle between Lent and Luxury, with their attendant hosts. The observation of Lent and other fast-days was a very important aspect of medieval eating habits, which went back to the early days of the Christian Church. The custom that only fish should be eaten on such days began as only one of a variety of practices adopted by the first Christians: 'Some abstained from all living creatures; others of all living creatures ate only fish; some ate fowls together with fish; others abstained from berries and eggs; others ate dry bread only; and some not so much as that.' Abstinence and moderation were the general rule, rather than any specific diet, though by St Augustine's time the avoidance of flesh was firmly established. He attacked those who observed the letter but not the spirit of Lent:

There are some observers of Lent that study deliciousness more than religion, and seek out new pleasures for the belly, more than how to chastise the concupiscence of the old man . . . They are afraid of any vessels in which flesh has been boiled, as if they were unclean; and yet in their own flesh fear not the luxury of the throat and the belly. These men fast, not to diminish their wonted voracity by temperance, but by deferring a meal to increase their immoderate greediness. For when the time of refreshment comes they rush to their plentiful tables as beasts to their manger, and stuff their bellies with great variety of artificial and strange sauces, taking in more by devouring than they are able to digest again by fasting.

He goes on to say that the fast is not observed properly if the abstinence of the day is spoiled by any immoderate indulgence of an evening banquet; much less did he esteem it a fast to dine upon delicacies as a substitute for the abstinence from flesh.

Despite such attacks on the change from flesh to fish 'or a more delicious food' as being merely 'a mock fast, and a mere innovation unknown to the ancients', the rule of fish only was firmly established in medieval Europe. Lent was no great harshness for the wealthy, who could afford fish or could hire a cook to make dishes which cunningly counterfeited meat by the use of vegetables; but for the poor, particularly in towns, it meant a change from a subsistence diet to one which was barely adequate to sustain life. The cookery books are full of versions of recipes marked 'for a fish day' which are just as luxurious as their equivalents for meat days. And although monastic good cheer is largely a legend put about by the monasteries' enemies, St Augustine would have had some sharp words for some of them, with well-stocked fishponds and cellars. The more worldly orders, in particular the Cluniac monks, were not averse to doing themselves well, in contrast to the spirit of the Rule of St Benedict, which provided the basis for life in the monasteries of western Europe. This forbade the eating of the flesh of quadrupeds, though even this was not strictly observed. In the eleventh century, the prior of Winchester had to wean his monks from meat by means of 'exquisite dishes of fish'; but by the thirteenth century the abbot was generally allowed meat at his table, and feast-days were treated as 'eatings of meat'. At the end of the twelfth century, Gerald of Wales found sixteen courses served up at a feast at Christ Church, Canterbury.

The overall effect of the Church's rules on diet was to make the cooking of fish more elaborate than it would otherwise have been. In one case, a new fish seems to have been imported into western Europe to meet the demand, the carp from eastern Germany. This gradually spread westwards during the fourteenth century, and became the stock item in many monastery fishponds. Like many other freshwater coarse fish, such as bream and pike, it is little eaten nowadays (the French pike rissole, *quenelle de brochet,* being the only important exception); but given the choice between the expensive monotony of salt fish or such fresh substitutes as could be caught locally, it is hardly surprising that it was a welcome addition to the menu.

Let us close our survey of Italian and French medieval cooking on a more cheerful note, with a great international banquet. The wedding ceremonies of Lionel Duke of Clarence, second son of Edward III, and Yolanda, daughter of Giangaleazzo Visconti, lord of Milan, were celebrated with especial pomp at Milan in 1368. Since, unlike so many medieval marriages, this was the wedding of two adults in person, rather than a child union or an affair of proxies, the presents and feast (which were interwoven in a splendid pageant) were more gorgeous than usual. Each course was accompanied by a gift, as the following list records:

FIRST COURSE
Golden sucking pigs with flames in their mouths, and gilded fish
Two leopards with velvet collars and silk leashes, and twelve couple of hounds

SECOND COURSE
Gilded hares and pike
Twelve couple of greyhounds with silk collars, gilded muzzles, and silk leashes with enamel buttons on them bearing the arms of the two lords, with pearl buttons at the end

THIRD COURSE
A gilded calf with gilded trout
Six alaunts (wolf-hounds) and six large hounds with velvet collars and gilded clasps

FOURTH COURSE
Golden quails and partridges with gilded 'remeri' (a kind of fish)
Twelve sparrowhawks and twelve brachets with trappings as before

FIFTH COURSE
Ducks, herons and carp, all golden
Peregrine falcons with the same trappings

SIXTH COURSE
Beef and chicken with garlic sauce, and sturgeon in stock
Twelve fine cuirasses and gauntlets with gilded clasps and fastenings
with the arms of the two lords

SEVENTH COURSE
Chickens and meat in limonia, *and tench likewise*
Twelve richly ornamented sets of jousting armour

EIGHTH COURSE
Beef, geese and pies of fat eels
Twelve sets of silver-mounted campaign armour with gilded arms of
the two lords

NINTH COURSE
Meat and fish en gelée
Ten pieces of gold cloth and ten pieces of silk

TENTH COURSE
Galantine of meat and galantine of lampreys
Two large barrels of malmsey and Greek wine, and six small barrels

ELEVENTH COURSE
Kid and small birds sprinkled with rose sugar and roasted with garlic
Six fine little coursers complete with harness, lances and shields

TWELFTH COURSE
*Hares and goats in ziverio [perhaps a sweet sauce] with another fish in the
same sauce*
Six large coursers equipped as before

THIRTEENTH COURSE
Venison and ox with frumenty and a purée of fish
Six fine little destriers with green velvet trappings

FOURTEENTH COURSE
Capons and hens in red and green sauce with oranges and a purée of tench
Six large jousting coursers with crimson velvet trappings

FIFTEENTH COURSE
Young pigeons, beans, salted tongue and carp

A mantle edged and lined with ermine, a doublet and a hat of satin, covered with pearls; then a mantle and a hat with panels embroidered with pearls

SIXTEENTH COURSE
Roast rabbits, peacocks, young ducks, and eels
A fine large basin of silver and two fine pieces of jewellery set with pearls, emeralds, sapphires and other gems, a diamond and pearl ring, five silver-gilt belts.

SEVENTEENTH COURSE
Junket and cheese
Twelve fine fat oxen

EIGHTEENTH COURSE
fruit
Two great coursers belonging to the count called Lion and Abbot.

Even the Renaissance at its most splendid would scarcely be able to match such an occasion: but before we go on to the extravagances of Burgundy under the Valois dukes and Rome under the Borghese popes, let us look first at England and Germany, and see how they took to these new Latin luxuries.

Early Medieval Recipes

Early medieval cookery is basically much simpler than that of ancient Rome, though complex dishes were occasionally made for special feasts. The ingredients for early medieval recipes are less exotic than those for Roman cookery. Perhaps the only items that will give difficulty are pine-kernels (see pp. 24–5 above) and saffron, which should be bought in powdered form. Verjuice, the juice of sour grapes, or crab-apples, is not readily available, but a very dry still cider and a little vinegar make an acceptable substitute, and this is given accordingly in the recipes.

LIMONIA [for 4 persons]

Chicken with lemon.

3 lb chicken

For stuffing
¼ pt milk
2 oz dates
2 pieces stem ginger

6 egg whites
4 oz pine kernels
3 crushed cloves

Pound the pine-kernels in a mortar, stone and chop the dates, and chop the stem ginger. Blend the milk and egg whites, and add the other ingredients. Put in a shallow uncovered dish or baking tray in the oven at Regulo 3, 320°, for about 30 minutes to dry the mixture. Take out and use this to stuff the chicken. Roast the chicken in the normal way, either on the spit or in the oven.

For sauce
1 glass dry white wine
2 oz pine-kernels
2 pieces stem ginger
¼ tsp cinnamon
¼ tsp mace

2 tsp vinegar
2 tsp sugar
2 egg yolks
juice of 2 lemons

Pound the pine-kernels and chop the stem ginger finely. Put these in the liquidizer and add the wine, cinnamon, mace, vinegar, lemon juice and sugar. Blend briefly. Add egg yolks, blend again until smooth. Put in a small saucepan and bring to the boil. Simmer for a short while until thick.

A Book of Cookery, c. 1300 (Italian)

LAYMUNIWYA [for 4 persons]

Chicken with lemon.

3 lb chicken	*¾ pt mutton stock*
3 medium onions	*½ tsp cinnamon*
½ lb leeks	*½ tsp ground coriander*
¼ lb carrots	*tsp chopped mint*
½ lb aubergines	*2 pieces chopped ginger*
tsp salt	*2 oz ground almonds*
juice of 2 lemons	*tsp dried mint*

Wash aubergines, make ¼-inch-deep slits lengthwise and rub in salt. Leave for 30 minutes, then slice and fry in oil until partly cooked. Slice onions and add to stock. Add aubergines, chopped leeks and chopped carrots to stock. Joint the chicken and add this also, together with the spices and chopped mint. Simmer gently for 40–50 minutes. When almost cooked, add the lemon juice, the ground almonds and the dried mint. Continue to simmer until liquid is slightly reduced and beginning to thicken.

Arabic recipe-book, 13th century

SARACEN STEW [for 6 persons]

(*Brodo sarta cenito*).

3½ lb chicken	*4 oz grapes*
1 chicken liver from the chicken	*3 oz prunes*
2 oz breadcrumbs	*1½ oz whole peeled almonds*
1½ glasses white wine	*4 oz dates*
1½ glasses dry cider	*salt*
dsp vinegar	*pepper*

Pre-soak the prunes overnight and boil for 10 minutes. Roast the chicken, either on a spit (50 minutes) or in a casserole in a moderate oven (Regulo Mark 5, 360°) for 50–60 minutes. When roasted, carve into six portions and place in casserole. Put the raw liver and bread-crumbs with the cider, vinegar and white wine into a liquidizer. Blend and pour over the chicken. Season. Bring slowly to the boil, add the stoned dates, pipped grapes and stoned prunes and almonds, and simmer for 5–6 minutes before serving.

A Book of Cookery, c. 1300 (Italian)

CRETONÉE DE POIS NOUVEAUX   [for 4 persons]

Stew with young peas.

2½ lb boiled chicken	*6 yolks of egg*
1½ lb peas (either frozen or fresh	*¾ tsp ground ginger*
young peas)	*pinch saffron*
½ pt milk	*½ pt water*
4 oz breadcrumbs	

Boil peas in salted water until very soft. Drain and mash, and fry in lard until slightly dry (about 5–6 minutes). Put milk in large saucepan and bring to boil. Remove from flame and stir in breadcrumbs. Add ginger, saffron and puréed peas. Quarter the chicken and brown lightly in lard. Add to the mixture and bring to the boil. Turn out into a large flat fireproof dish and continue to simmer. Drop the yolks of egg in to the dish from a height, so that they break and spread; form a pattern round the edge of the dish in this way. Continue to simmer until the yolks are cooked, and serve.

Viandier de Taillevent, c. 1380

GRAVÉ   [for 4 persons]

'A stew for winter.'

2½ lb chicken	*2 thick slices white bread*
1½ pts beef stock	*½ tsp ginger*
3 crushed cloves	*½ tsp cinnamon*
½ lb onions	*2 glasses dry cider*
pepper	*1 dsp vinegar*
2½ glasses dry white wine	

Roast chicken in moderate oven (Regulo Mark 5, 360°) for 50 minutes. Peel and chop onions. Take a 3-pint casserole and fry onions in this over very low heat in a little oil, until transparent but not brown, turning frequently. Put the bread to soak in the beef stock. When the chicken is cooked, take it out of the oven and quarter it. Add the quarters to the onions. Mix the spices, cider, vinegar and wine. Purée the bread and stock through a sieve. Add the mixed spices and liquid and the bread and stock to the chicken and onions. Bring to the boil and simmer for 10 minutes before serving.

Le Menagier de Paris, c. 1400

SAUCE FOR A ROAST CHICKEN

6 oz flaked almonds	*4 pieces stem ginger*
2½ glasses dry cider	*1 dsp vinegar*
½ pt meat stock	

Chop the stem ginger finely, and mix with the remaining ingredients. Put in a medium saucepan and bring to the boil. Simmer for 5 minutes and serve as a separate sauce.

Maino Mainerio, c. 1340

CHICKEN STUFFED WITH ORANGES [for 6 persons]

3½ lb chicken	*2 pieces stem ginger*
2½ glasses dry cider	*1½ glasses dry white wine*
1 dsp vinegar	*pepper*
salt	*2 oranges*

Slice the oranges into rounds, throwing away the top and bottom rounds. Boil in the wine, cider and vinegar for about 5 minutes. Add the ginger, season well, and stuff the chicken with these. Any surplus pieces can be put into a pan with the water in which the chicken is to be boiled. Boil the chicken for 45–50 minutes. Drain and carve; the stuffing should not be eaten, as its function is simply to flavour the chicken meat.

Le Menagier de Paris, c. 1400

VEAL 'À LA CHARPIE' [For 4 persons]

1½ lb stewing veal	*6 eggs*
¼ lb lard	*pepper, salt*

Parboil the veal in a large pan, in 2 pints salted water. Cut in pieces and fry in lard in a large frying pan. Beat the eggs thoroughly, and when the meat is just brown, pour eggs over meat. Simmer until cooked, and sprinkle with pepper.

Traité de cuisine, c. 1300

PORK STEW [for 4 persons]

2 lb leg of pork (boned)	*1 slice slightly burnt brown toast*
½ lb onions	*stock from pork*
¼ tsp pepper	*icing sugar*
¼ tsp mace	*¼ tsp ginger*
¼ tsp cinnamon	

Chop pork into square pieces, and boil in salted water for 20–25 minutes. Slice the onions and fry in lard in a large pan. When the pork is cooked, take out the meat, strain the stock and add the spices to the stock. Crumble the toast into the sauce and strain through a sieve again. Add the stock to the onions and bring to the boil, stirring well. Dust the pork with icing sugar and pour the sauce over before serving.

Traité de cuisine, c. 1300

CHICKEN BROTH À LA PROVENÇALE [for 4 persons]

(*Brodo dei capponi a la provenzale*).

Giblets of two chickens, or ¼ lb chicken livers	¾ pt boiling water
	¼ tsp cinnamon
2 eggs	¼ tsp mace
¼ tsp pepper	salt to taste

Fry giblets or livers lightly in oil. Drain, put in saucepan and add boiling water. Add spices and salt. Bring to boil, break eggs and drop in. Stir well, simmering for about 5 minutes.

A Book of Cookery, c. 1300 (Italian)

ONION STEW [for 4 persons]

2 lb onions	¼ tsp cinnamon
½ lb soft cream cheese	¾ lb chopped stewing steak
3 eggs	pinch saffron
1 tsp pepper	¾ tsp ginger

Slice the onions and rinse in colander under hot tap. Drain and cook in oil in a frying pan or casserole with the meat, cheese, pepper and other spices. Beat the eggs, and when the mixture is almost cooked, add the eggs and more pepper to taste. Continue to cook until the eggs are done, and serve.

A Book of Cookery, c. 1300 (Italian)

PEAS WITH MEAT [for 4 persons]

(*Piselli con carne*).

1 lb peas	4 oz bacon
¾ lb mutton off bone	¼ pt water
salt, pepper	pinch saffron

Boil peas in salted water until just cooked. Drain and put in fresh water with bacon, mutton and saffron. Season. Bring to the boil and simmer until meat is cooked (about 15–20 minutes). Serve.

A Book of Cookery, c. 1300 (Italian)

HARICOT DE MOUTON   [for 6 persons]

1½ lb mutton, off bone   *2 tsp chopped parsley*
6 medium onions   *tsp chopped sage*
1 pt strong beef stock   *¼ tsp pepper*
½ pt dry cider   *1 tbs vinegar*
½ tsp cinnamon   *¼ tsp ginger*
2 tbs oil

Chop the onions finely, and cut the mutton into 2-inch cubes. Fry both in oil, until meat is lightly browned. Add beef stock, parsley and sage, and bring to the boil. Simmer for 5–6 minutes; add spices, cider and vinegar and continue to simmer for a further 10 minutes.

Viandier de Taillevent, c. 1380

'A SUBTLE ENGLISH STEW'   [for 4 persons]

1 lb peeled chestnuts   *¼ pt water*
8 yolks of hard-boiled eggs   *½ tsp pepper*
½ lb liver   *pinch saffron*

Chop the chestnuts, egg yolks and liver. Put the chestnuts and liver into the water in a medium saucepan and bring to the boil. Simmer for 10–12 minutes before adding the egg yolks, saffron and pepper. Simmer for a further 2–3 minutes and serve.

Viandier de Taillevent, c. 1380

SOUPE À L'OIGNON   [for 4 persons]
Onion soup.

1 lb onions   *¼ pt dry still cider*
½ lb peas   *4 oz butter*
1 dsp vinegar   *2 pts salted water*

Slice onions thinly, and cook in a large casserole in butter, adding a little water to stop them burning. Bring ½ pt salted water to the boil in a medium saucepan, add the peas and cook for 5–10 minutes until completely soft. Drain and purée in liquidizer. Add purée, cider, vinegar and 1½ pts salted water to onions in casserole and simmer for 30 minutes.

Printed edition of Taillevent, 15th century

GRAMOSE [for 4 persons]

This is a kind of custard sauce for use with slices of cold meat. The sauce should be allowed to cool and then poured over the meat. Do not allow to boil, or the eggs will scramble.

4–6 eggs   *1½ glasses dry still cider*
1 tsp vinegar   *¼ pt stock*

Beat eggs, both yolk and white, until liquid. Beat in cider, vinegar and stock. Put mixture in a medium saucepan, and continue to beat until almost at boiling point. Pour at once into a cold container, allow to cool, and pour over slices of meat.

Le Menagier de Paris, c. 1400

HOUSSEBARRE DE CHAR [for 2 persons]

A variation on *gramose* (above), which is slightly easier to make and perhaps more palatable to modern tastes. The meat can be heated lightly under the grill and the sauce poured over it hot if preferred.

4 egg yolks   *1 glass white wine*
6 tbs stock   *1 dsp vinegar*
1 glass dry still cider

Beat eggs 'until you are bored' (*tant comme à ennuy*). Add stock, cider, vinegar and wine, and put in saucepan. Bring slowly to boil, continuing to beat. Pour over meat and serve; or allow to cool for use with cold meat.

Le Menagier de Paris, c. 1400

BROUET VERT D'OEUFS ET DE FROMAGE [for 4 persons]

('A green stew of eggs and cheese').

This shows the medieval love of disguising ingredients; eggs and cheese are predominantly yellow, so they are transformed into a green dish.

2 oz parsley   *½ tsp powdered ginger*
½ pt stock   *4 eggs*
½ pt salted water   *2 slices brown bread*
4 oz grated cheese   *½ lb peas*
pinch saffron   *1 tbs white wine*
½ tsp sage

Soak bread in ¼ pt stock. Moisten powdered ginger in wine. Bring ½ pt salted water to boil in a medium saucepan, add the peas and cook for 5–10 minutes until completely soft. Drain and purée in liquidizer. Mash bread, mix with saffron, purée half the cheese, remaining stock, sage, and parsley in liquidizer, and blend. Stir in ginger, and pour into medium saucepan. Bring to the boil, stirring gently. Meanwhile, poach eggs in boiling salted water and drain. Simmer mixture for 10 minutes, then add eggs and sprinkle with grated cheese before serving. The result should be a contrast of bright green and yellow.

Le Menagier de Paris, c. 1400

IFLAGUN

This was a dish taken over by the Arabs from the Crusaders and Armenians; it looks from its contents as though the Crusaders learnt it in the Near East.

½ *roll per person, slightly*	*grated cheese*
hollowed out	*rue*
1 egg per person	*spices as given below, in small*
	quantities

Break egg into bowl, add salt, crushed pepper, ginger, aniseed, caraway and cumin. The pepper should predominate, to give 'heat' to the dish; the original also includes hemp, sesame and poppy seed. Mix the spices thoroughly with the egg and add a little rue and grated cheese. Spread the mixture on the roll, and cook under the grill. 'This recipe is excellent,' says the Arab writer.

Arabic recipe-book, 13 century

GRAVÉ OF PRAWNS   [for 6 persons]

The original is for crayfish; scampi would also be suitable.

2 lb peeled prawns	*6 tbs vinegar*
6 oz peas	*tsp ginger*
3 oz ground almonds	*½ tsp cinnamon*
2 thick slices white bread	*3 crushed cloves*
1 pt beef stock	

Put prawns in salted water and bring to boil. Simmer for 4–5 minutes, then drain and put aside in covered dish to keep warm. Bring ½ pt salted water to boil in a medium saucepan, add the peas and cook for 5–10 minutes until completely soft. Drain and purée in liquidizer. Add bread, beef stock and spices and blend thoroughly. Put in medium saucepan, add vinegar and bring to boil, stirring thoroughly. When boiling, stir in ground almonds. Serve in individual dishes, with prawns sprinkled on top of sauce.

Le Menagier de Paris, c. 1400

BLANC MANGIER EN CARESME [for 4 persons]

½ *lb rice*	*3 qts water*
slice lemon	*dsp salt*
2 oz ground almonds	½ *tsp cinnamon*
½ *tsp ginger*	½ *pt milk*
1 tbs sugar	*whole fried almonds for decoration*

Bring 3 qts water to boil with slice of lemon and dsp salt. Add rice, boil for 15 minutes, allowing to boil fiercely. Drain at once. Meanwhile, fry almonds in oil in small frying pan. Mix almonds and milk. Add to rice and liquidize. Serve powdered with spices and studded with fried almonds.

Le Menagier de Paris, c. 1400

CRISPELLI OR FRITELLE UBALDINE [for 4 persons]

A kind of pancake.

3 oz flour	*3 eggs*
pinch powdered saffron	*2 oz clarified lard*
sugar and honey to taste	

Sift flour into a bowl and break in eggs one at a time, drawing in the flour as each egg is put in. Add saffron and beat for 2–3 minutes. Take a medium frying pan, melt the lard and pour in enough mixture to cover centre. Fry until light brown, turning as necessary. Eat with sugar and honey to taste.

A Book of Cookery, c. 1300 (Italian)

Figure 4 A feast at the end of the fifteenth-century: King Arthur and his court from a woodcut of 1498. The details of the table have changed very little by comparison with the twelfth-century feast on page 36.

The north of Europe was slow to adopt the gastronomic delights discovered by its southern neighbours, viewing such extravagances with deep suspicion. Among the reasons why Edward II's Gascon favourite, Piers Gaveston, was distrusted were the luxurious habits into which he led the king when the latter was still Prince of Wales; and as if to confirm the English nobles' doubts, two gilded forks of the kind that had so horrified Peter Damian at Venice were found among his possessions after his banishment. And almost before these new-fangled ideas had had a chance to establish themselves, the English kings were busily trying to restrain luxurious habits by passing laws against excessive show. Just as Philip the Fair had enacted in 1294 that no family should have more than soup and two main dishes for supper, so Edward III echoed him in 1336:

No man shall cause himself to be served in his house or elsewhere at dinner, other meal or supper, or at any other time, with more than two courses, and each mess of two sorts of victuals at the utmost, be it flesh or fish, with the common sorts of pottage, without sauce or any other sort of victuals, and if any man choose to have sauce for his mess, he well may, provided it be not made at great cost; and if flesh or fish are to be mixed therein, it shall be of two sorts only at the utmost, either fish or flesh, and shall stand instead of a mess.

And in 1363 the diet of servants was limited by law to flesh and fish once a day, the rest to be of other victuals such as milk, butter and cheese, 'according to their estate'.

However, it was not only extravagant living but also the extravagances of politics, in the shape of a newly begun war with France, that dictated these restrictions. The king and the Black Prince themselves were not the best of examples in economy, and English writers were readier to criticize such habits than their French counterparts. In the poem *Winner and Waster*, written about 1352, the failure of the king to balance his way of life between getting (winning) and spending (wasting) is attacked. The poet depicts a rich feast, which Winner scathingly attacks as unnecessary; but Waster argues that such spending is needed in order to give employment to the poor, and is only fitting to a lord's rank:

Wouldst thou have lords to live as lads a-foot?
Prelates as priests that parishes guard?

> Proud merchants of price, as pedlars o' the village?
> Let lords live as they list, lads as befits them –
> These the bacon and beef, these bitterns and swans
> These the rough of the rye, these the ruddy wheat,
> These the gray gruel, these the good sauce.
> So may the people have their part, now in poverty bestead,
> Some good morsel of meat to mend their ill cheer.

And anyway, Waster adds, are we to let all nature's resources go unused, and stop hunting and hawking after game? That would only serve to increase the price of other food, and the poor would be even worse off. But Edward III, despite the huge ransom extracted from John the Good after Poitiers, failed to balance his getting and spending, like most medieval monarchs, and the debate, as in the poem, remained unresolved.

Richard II, abandoning the pursuit of the French crown, came down firmly in favour of wasting. Inheriting none of his father's and grandfather's military tastes, he took after Edward II in his love of luxury, but in rather more positive terms. Under him, the English court became one of the most glittering in Europe, a Mecca for artists and men of letters, craftsmen and purveyors of rarities. Richard himself loved costly books, romances in rich bindings, as much as the poets whose works he encouraged; and his taste in dress was equally showy: here is a pen-portrait from an allegorical poem that might be the king himself:

> Embroidered all with gold coins and beryls full rich
> His collar with chalcedonies clustered full thick
> With many diamonds full dear sewn on his sleeves
> The seams were with sapphires set in great number
> With emeralds and amethysts upon each side
> With richest of rubies edged at the hems.

Another source of inspiration could have been the mantle presented to Richard's uncle Lionel of Clarence by Giangaleazzo Visconti; and Richard's taste in banquets has more than a passing similarity to the products of the Visconti kitchen. Fortunately for us, the notebook of his master cook has survived, on the end of a roll of royal accounts. *The Forme of Cury* is the earliest English cookery book, containing just under two hundred recipes; but its contents

Figure 5 A sixteenth-century woodcut showing a roast peacock served with head and tail feathers as the centrepiece of a feast. This was a medieval custom which lasted on special occasions into the nineteenth-century.

are very far from being the 'roast beef of old England'. To start with, meat is rarely, if ever, served whole, but is teased into pâtés or fricassees, while the ingredients betray a southern origin: olive oil rather than butter (which could be used only in cool climates because it would turn rancid too easily), raisins of Corinth, Lombard mustard, and Greek and Sicilian wines such as malmsey and vernage.

As we look at the most typical dishes, mawmenny, frumenty, caudle, dariols or *blanc manger*, it is clear that although traces of a simpler English cooking survive, the keynote is a search for novelty which would have delighted Apicius, treats for jaded palates. There is the same element of elaborate disguise of ingredients reminiscent of Apicius's 'and no one will know what they are eating', though some of the treatment is due to the absence of forks. Gaveston's forks were probably used for extracting preserves from their pots, a miniature version of the cook's meat hook in the cauldron, and were certainly not for individual use at table. On the other hand, refinement frowned on the knife, fingers and bread method of eating, which required at the very least frequent washing of hands and clean towels: so instead of soiling their fingers as they picked the meat off the bones, Richard and his court probably used spoons to eat these new dishes, in which the meat was reduced to a manageable consistency in the kitchen.

For the first time the presentation of food was regarded from an aesthetic point of view. Even the Romans at their most luxurious had tended to ignore the actual appearance of a dish, unless it was to present it in a grotesque disguise, as the living animal or in some quite unexpected form, as at Trimalchio's feast in Petronius's *Satyricon*. A fairly universal greyness prevailed at their tables as a result. But now dishes were coloured with saffron and horse-parsley to relieve the monotony, and sometimes gilded (as at the Visconti feast) or stained with sandalwood, while special display pieces or 'subtleties' made of marzipan or jelly decorated the table at the end of each course. These were probably edible at first, but soon became a kind of art-form in themselves, often made of inedible materials.

As for the ingredients, there was the same insistence on spices which characterized Italian and French cooking of the period, and which has led so many modern commentators to turn up their noses at these recipes: 'It goes without saying that food of the sort just cited is revolting to modern taste,' says W. E. Mead in his otherwise excellent book on *The English Medieval Feast*. This is true only if one is allergic to spices. We accept much continental and eastern cookery which is more highly spiced than medieval dishes, ignoring the fact that spices can be used in subtle combinations and small amounts. Much of the medieval cook's skill lay in this precise blending, and it is unfortunate that no 'cook's hints' survive on the use of the flavours in the manner of the advice given on buying meat in *The Parisian Housekeeper*. The recipes themselves are too vague to give us much clue, and skill in flavouring must be acquired at the cost of a few unpalatable experiments. For instance, the sauce for mutton given on p. 94 appears at first to be rather like French mustard, using ground ginger instead of mustard powder. But the result is quite unpalatable, and only if we substitute stem ginger pounded by hand does the recipe make sense. Moderation and the milder alternative are the keynote in interpreting a medieval recipe, together with a careful eye for anachronisms such as the use of malt vinegar instead of wine vinegar. Furthermore, in view of the relatively high cost of spices as reflected in account rolls of the period, no very great quantity could have been used in any one dish: a cook who poured half the contents of the spice-cupboard into one meal would soon have been sent back to turning the spit. And the earliest surviving spice-cupboards are on a very modest scale when one considers how large the households which they supplied were.

Sugar, as in the French and Italian recipes, was much used as a decoration, even on meat dishes, in its powdered form. In the early thirteenth century, it had been very scarce indeed; in 1226, Henry III directed the mayor of Winchester, the second largest city in the kingdom, to send him three pounds of Alexandria sugar; failing this, he was to send Buza sugar instead, if as much as three pounds could be found in the entire town. By the late fourteenth century, all this had changed and the royal kitchens were well supplied (at a price), though directions to take a 'great quantity' of sugar should still be interpreted in ounces rather than pounds. Much of the sugar was in the form of white powder (*poudre blanche*), ground down from the big sugar loaves in which it was transported, and not unlike icing sugar.

The Forme of Cury is an exceptional work in that it comes directly from the royal household at a period when cookery was held in high esteem. For a more commonplace view of English cookery, we must turn to the collections of recipes of the fifteenth century. There are several of these, none of them very long. They cannot be assigned to definite sources, but probably come from large households; quantities are sometimes for as many as forty helpings. They are all in English, now the common language of the realm instead of Anglo-French, and if there is none of the really scarce ingredients, there are still dishes in the tradition of *The Forme of Cury*. The materials used are, as before, rarely presented at table in their natural form, and the cook is still admired for his transformation of the raw substance:

> These cooks, how they stamp and strain and grind
> And turn their substance into accident
> Out of the hard bones they will knock
> The marrow (for nothing's thrown away)
> That slips down the throat so soft and sweet.
> Of spicery, of leaf and bark and root
> Shall be their sauces made, by delight
> To make us a still fresher appetite.

The main source of meat still remained the pig, fattened on acorns in the country or on slops in the towns. Despite the efforts of the city officials, the pigs of London still wandered loose in the streets of the capital in the fourteenth century. After the pig, cattle and sheep provided the bulk of the butcher's wares. Game was a delicacy for the tables of noblemen and the great monasteries; the latter received it as part of their tithes. Poultry was surprisingly expensive: a swan cost as much as a whole pig, a pheasant as much as a sheep.

Dairy produce, milk, cheese and butter, was largely regarded as unsuitable for use in elaborate cookery. If milk does appear, it is almost always as a basis for almonds, while olive oil or lard were preferred to butter. On the other hand, some of the confections invented by noblemen's cooks were becoming more widely available: wafers and gingerbread were on sale in the London streets, as was garlic. The French were already renowned for their consumption of it, but in England it was rarely used except as a sauce for goose.

How was all this brought to the table? We have a menu for the dinner given by Sir John Cornwell to Henry V early in the fifteenth century which can be explained by reference to the cookery books. Each course consisted of a number of dishes presented at the same time; there is much greater variety within the courses than at the Visconti wedding feast, but this was a less lavish occasion and whereas the Milanese provided enough of each dish for all the guests, here the diners evidently took their choice of each set of dishes:

First course 'in prandio': frumenty with venison, blanc manger, beef and mutton, cygnets, fat capons, veal, herons, baked venison, 'leche ffloree' [slices of meat in a sauce]

Second course: numbles [lights of venison], meat jelly, pheasant, sucking pig, kid, pigeons, partridges, roast venison, baked white custards, meat slices in white [almond] sauce; fried sambucade [elder flower cakes]

Third course: royal mawmenny, pear preserve, rabbits, bitterns, egrets, plovers, quails, spoonbills, small birds, larks, puff pastry, 'leche lumbarde' [a kind of pork sausage in a sauce], fried crisp pancakes

Fourth course 'in cena': spit-roasted venison, boiled cream, sucking pig in sage sauce, shoulders of mutton, fat capons, herons, partridges, baked chickens, fried sliced meat

Last course: cold cream, jelly, roast venison, roast kid, rabbits, pigeons, egrets, quails, small birds, baked custard pies, damascus slices [perhaps a sweetmeat]

The notes '*in prandio*' (for dinner) and '*in cena*' (for supper) indicate that this was a feast which included both dinner and supper, perhaps continuously! All that is lacking is the selection of subtleties which usually ended the course, bearing a motto which explained their meaning, often related to the particular occasion of the feast: all those at Henry V's coronation feast contained allusions to St Catherine in honour of the queen.

The variety and number of fifteenth-century cookery books in England is due to the style of cooking developed at Richard II's court which quickly became an English tradition. All the surviving books contain a number of recipes from *The Forme of Cury*. One entertaining work in verse, *Liber cure cocorum* (*The Book of the Cooks' Art*), written about 1420, opens with a series of practical jokes to be played on the cook. Among these are how to make meat seem raw when it is in fact cooked, how to make meat look as though it is infested by worms (by shredding pieces of gut over it) and how to spoil his stock (by adding soap so that it froths over). This simple humour is matched by the simple rhyme in which the recipes are set out, though it is interesting to see how the French names for the dishes are retained. Most of the offerings come from *The Forme of Cury* and from another collection written in 1381; but such items as tansy cake and haggis make their first appearances here. Tansy remained a popular flavouring until the eighteenth century, but later uses of it were generally with apples (recipe, p. 94). Haggis is usually thought of as a Scottish dish, but the earliest references to it are all to be found in English books. The name is probably derived from 'hagging' or hacking the meat into mince, and for once it is a native dish without a French equivalent, so this is one of the first purely English recipes. It was not until the eighteenth century that it became a speciality found only in Scotland, for as late as 1669 an English cook could write about, 'The Haggis or Haggas, of whose goodness it is in vain to boast, because there is hardly to be found a man that doth not affect them'. The method of cookery given in *Liber cure cocorum* scarcely differs from the modern recipe, except that the herbs – hyssop and savory – are more pungent, and the kidneys are to be 'on the *tourbillon* made'. What this early kitchen gadget with a French name was like can only be guessed at; literally, it means a whirlwind, so it may have been a special fast rotating spit.

Two other cookery books in plain English prose appeared soon after this, between 1430 and 1450. Again, the dishes are mainly derived from *The Forme of Cury*, though tansy reappears and there are such delightfully named concoctions as hanoney, sturmye and pokerounce along with more homely fare like cabbages and whelks. The exotic dishes were new imports from France, as the pine-kernels used in pokerounce show. It is not unlike the toasted nuts and honey of the Roman cooks, though the use of white bread as if it were a kind of cake betrays its medieval date (recipe p. 98). Sturmye, a kind of sweet and sour pork in white sauce, and hanoney, made of eggs and onions, seem to be native inventions (p. 92). Cokyntryce is pure fantasy, a kind of subtlety made of meat, as befits a dish named after the fabulous creature hatched from a cock's egg which could kill a man with its eyes: this recipe comes from Dorothy Hartley's *Food in England*, using chicken and rabbit instead of capon and sucking pig:

Dress the boiling fowl whole, but dress the rabbit by removing head and front legs completely and setting the hind-legs out flat. Now truss the ribs of the rabbit well into the rib cage of the fowl, slitting the fowl's vent and skewering the fowl legs back over the body of the rabbit. Tie into shape and simmer gently, till quite tender; leave it to grow cold in the stock. Next day, lift out, remove string, and drain; stuff with forcemeat, and roast till dry and brown, and the forcemeat cooked. Again leave to cool. When ready to serve, glaze the whole with bright dark glaze, picking out the shape with powdered egg yolk. As it is a 'show dish' it should be made specially decorative, with cut beet, egg white etc.

Set it high on a nest of green parsley, add a small carved head, with scarlet leather, or gilded cock's comb at the cock end; set the two wings either side the body, and display the four legs (with gilded claws) out behind. A gold egg between the paws, or gilded skewers, or anything decorative, may be added, and a 'collar' of cut parchment or of plaited straws should be put around the neck of the wooden head. The 'joint' should be arranged upon a wooden board, both for appearance and for ease in carving.

For the forcemeat: a usual mixture, but add a good lining of chopped fat ham before the forcemeat is pressed in (this helps to baste the cockatrice while roasting); spice the filling rather highly, as it is to be eaten cold.

For the glaze: the usual aspic glaze may be used; ... a quick substitute may be made by dissolving a jelly foundation with 2 tablespoonfuls of best vinegar and meat extract. It need not be clear, if it sets with a fine bright glaze. Brush on rather thickly, till well coated, and pour the final glaze over the last, quite liquid, to get a good finish.

But for the full complications of the medieval kitchen it is hard to beat the dish known as 'appraylere', pork *appareillé* or dressed. Here is a modern translation, otherwise unaltered, of the original instructions:

Take lean pork meat and boil it well: and when it is boiled, chop it small; then take saffron, ginger, cinnamon, salt, galingale [a variety of ginger], old cheese, breadcrumbs, and pound them small in a mortar; put the meat in with the spices, and see that it is well ground. Moisten it with raw eggs. Then take a long pitcher, rinse it thoroughly all round [rub lard all round it], remove any surplus lard. Fill the pitcher with the stuffing, take a piece of clean canvas and fold it until it is just big enough to cover the mouth. Tie the canvas to the rim of the pitcher, and put it in to boil as though it were a large joint, in a lead dish or a cauldron. Take the pitcher and break it, and extract the stuffing. Prepare a spit, broach it and put it before the fire to roast. Make a good batter of spicery, saffron, galingale, cinnamon and flour, grind it small in a mortar, moisten with raw eggs and add enough sugar of Alexandria. As the stuffing dries, baste it with batter and serve it up when cooked.

A simpler version of this, called 'golden apples' (*powme dorys*) will befound on p. 91.

All these collections came from noble households, and the repetition of various items in very similar forms in the different books implies that very few cooks would have known them, let alone have attempted them. In any case, the manuscripts would have been kept well away from the grease and smoke of the kitchen, and were probably used by the chamberlain or officer of the household responsible for arranging the meals in order to brief the cook, who probably could not read them in any case. This is one of the reasons why quantities are never given. Furthermore, there is a large gap in the series of cookery books after 1450, perhaps reflecting the troubled times of the Wars of the Roses and the decline of the great noble households. The next English book is *A Proper Newe Book of Cookerye* printed in 1545, aimed at a very different audience.

So the impetus of Richard II's love of luxury had petered out by the middle of the following century; but cookery continued to be regarded as a new-fangled art by many people. John Russell, writing his *Book of Nurture*, on education and household matters, in the mid-fifteenth century, echoes the verses quoted earlier, though with a gloomier turn:

Cooks with their new conceits, chopping, straining, stamping and
    grinding,
Many new dishes all day they are contriving and finding,
That provoketh the people to perils of passage through pain
    tormenting,
And through sheer excess of such receits, of their life to make
    an ending.

From this period onwards, a new aspect of food comes to the fore, the art of its presentation at table. Carving had always been an important function at feasts, but it now began to be regarded as a skill in its own right. Juvenal's 'carver prancing about' of Roman days reappears, but he now has detailed written instructions on how to set about his task, along with the other servants involved in the preparation of the banquet. There was a great deal of ceremonial involved: dishes had to be paraded before the host, and clean towels, basins and ewers brought at the appropriate moment. The carver had to know which guests to serve first, and to whom the choicest bits of each dish were to be given. He was also expected to discover guests' preferences and to cater for them accordingly. Finally, he had to know all the appropriate terms for dealing with the different meats, poultry and game. A list of these was among the earliest books to be printed in England, by Wynkyn de Worde. It begins with 'Termes of a kerver': 'Breke that dere, lesche [slice] that brawne [meat], rare that goose, lyft that swanne, sauce that capon, spoyle that henne, frusshe that chekyn, unbrace that malarde, unlace that cony, dysmembre that heron, dysplaye that crane, dysfygure that pecocke.'

It continues with items which we should not regard as being 'carved' at all today: 'Tyere that egge, chyne that samon, strynge that lampreye, splatte that pyke, sauce that playce, splayce that breme, syde that haddocke, tuske that barbell, culpon that troute, undertraunche that purpos [porpoise], barbe that lopster.' But these were the trappings of great occasions. Most meals, and the banquets of many lesser lords, must have come nearer to the freeman's feast described by John Russell in the *Book of Nurture*:

> A freeman may feast as befits his station
> Flesh with mustard is suitable
>   Bacon served with peas.
>
> Beef or stewed mutton's serviceable
> Boiled chicken or capon agreeable
>   Depending on the season.
>
> Roasted geese or pig are profitable
> Capon pie and custard tasteable
>   If eggs and cream are handy.
>
> For this homely fare is suitable
> Mortrewes or jussell are delectable
>   For the second course, and these:

Some veal or lamb, kid or rabbit
Chicken or pigeon roasted on the spit
Bakemeats or doucets within reason.

Then after that fritters and sliced meat
At the right time such dishes are meet
To serve both in chamber and hall.

Then apples and pears with delicate spices
After the turn of the year such fruit suffices
With bread and cheese as well.

Spiced cakes and wafers worthily
Go with bragot and mead; thus men may merrily
Please well both great and small.

In contrast to what we can discover about the English style of cooking in the Middle Ages, there is little more than a footnote to be added about German cookery. Germany never seems to have developed a definite tradition in the same way as fifteenth-century England, unless it is buried in the handful of unpublished manuscripts which contain monastic recipes. Only one important secular cookery book has survived, *Ein buch von guoter spise* (*A Book of Good Food*), which probably comes from northern Bavaria at the end of the fourteenth century, that is, about the same date as *The Forme of Cury*. Even though it is almost certainly the court cookery book of a German prince, the dishes are for the most part simple and homely fare. One or two Italian dishes do appear, such as the two recipes '*à la grecque*'. A recipe for a dish of liver ends up, surprisingly, as an accompaniment for game or fish, a kind of early pâté to be eaten as a side dish. A 'konkavelite' is a kind of rice, almond and cherry cake of the rather heavy kind favoured by medieval cooks, not unlike the recipe for cherries from an English source given on p. 96; as the Germans were renowned for their heavy drinking, the extra starchiness of this dessert may have been intended to absorb some of the liquid! The only ingredients which stand out from the usual range of almonds, rice and spices are beer and butter; beer is used in a dish of beans (p. 95), and a fruit turnover is to be fried in butter (p. 98). Beer was much used in later German domestic cooking, and appears occasionally in English cookery from the late sixteenth century onwards; butter becomes

7. A medieval cook with his cooking pot, showing the fork used to handle the meat and the adjustable rack from which the pot hung. From a thirteenth-century French manuscript.

8. The Land of Cockaigne: Pieter Brueghel's vision of the medieval dreamworld of plenty where food does not have to be won by toil and sweat.

9. A great lord at table, with his carver, sewer (holding the cup), and two musicians. A fourteenth-century English illustration of the parable of Dives and Lazarus.

10. Preparing and serving a meal in a rich fifteenth-century household.

increasingly important not only in England and Germany but in French cooking after the mid-seventeenth century.

A few menus for great feasts survive, but these do not show any particular tendency towards special local dishes; this is the bill of fare for the enthronement of the bishop of Strassburg in 1440, in which the most interesting feature is the appearance of cabbage:

First service: cabbage, boiled beef, ragoût of white almonds garnished with chicken [perhaps a *blanc manger*], fish in aspic, flans filled with pâté

Second service: wild boar stew, venison pâté, cranes boiled in caramel sauce, ornamented pastry, blanc manger

Third service: sugared rice, capons, chickens and sucking pigs, roasted poultry and veal jelly with sauce, pears in pastry, plum preserve, dessert

Otherwise we glean only glimpses of diet in medieval Germany from monastic chronicles or courtly romances. From the monks we learn of salad at a south German monastery as early as the ninth century (though raw herbs must have been a frequent dish when times were hard) and foreign fish, lemons and figs at another south German monastery in 1075; the chronicler at Colmar in 1380 was horrified by a new fashion in food: 'People began to eat frogs, a dish considered abominable until the present day.' As to courtly food, it seems to have been the usual princely menu as found in Europe before the new Italian ideas crept in: chicken and game were highly regarded, veal and beef despised. The peacock was used as a centrepiece here as well, despite its tough dry flesh. Many varieties of fish, chiefly freshwater, were eaten: salmon, trout, eel, pike and lampreys are mentioned. The range of sauces was restricted: a pepper sauce accompanied venison, peacock and pike. Side dishes and dessert are rarely if ever described, and there is no widespread evidence for the use of decorative pastries and subtleties. However, humbler poets describe two traditional German traits from a very early period: a love for sausages, which were made in great variety from pork, beef and game, and for drinking, with which large meals usually ended.

English and German Medieval Court Recipes

(The recipes are English unless it is explicitly stated that they are German.)

BLANC MANGER [for 4 persons]

3lb cooked chicken
3 oz ground almonds
¾ pt milk
6 oz rice (not *long grain, which is a later variety*)

2 oz sugar
3 qts boiling water ⎫
4 tsp salt   ⎬ for rice
1 oz flaked almonds ⎭

Carve the chicken and dice the meat. Steam rice by cooking for 10 minutes in rapidly boiling salted water. Drain rice. Meanwhile, mix ground almonds and milk into a smooth paste. Add to rice in a saucepan and bring to the boil. Add the diced chicken meat, and simmer very gently until the mixture thickens. Fry the flaked almonds in a little oil in a small frying pan until just brown. Pour the chicken and rice into a serving dish and stir in the sugar. Drain the flaked almonds and sprinkle over the dish before serving.

c. 1380

GELYNE IN DUBATTE [for 4 persons]

2½ lb chicken
¾ pt chicken stock
1½ glasses wine
3 crushed cloves
1 tbs wine vinegar

¼ tsp pepper
¼ tsp cinnamon
2 slices white bread
½ tsp ground mace

Roast chicken in moderate oven (Regulo 5, 360°) until almost cooked but not browned (about 45—50 minutes). Joint the chicken and put into a casserole. Add the chicken stock, wine, spices, vinegar and roughly crumbled bread, bring to the boil and simmer for about 10 minutes, stirring gently, before serving.

c. 1430

MORTREWS BLANK

¾ lb minced cold pork
3 oz ground almonds
1½ oz rice flour
2 tbs sugar

¾ lb minced cold chicken
2 pts chicken stock
1 tsp ground ginger

Mix the minced pork and chicken thoroughly together with a fork. Stir the ground almonds into the stock, then add the rice flour and beat until smooth. Put the meat and the other mixture into a large saucepan and bring to the boil, stirring well. Simmer for 10–15 minutes, until the mixture thickens. Pour into a serving dish and powder with a mixture of ginger and sugar.

c. 1380

PORK IN WHITE WINE [for 4 persons]

The name *vyne grace* given to this recipe indicates that one of the Greek white wines was used in it; these were much appreciated in the Middle Ages.

1 lb cold pork
1 tbs vinegar
¼ tsp ginger
1 tbs sugar

½ pt dry white wine (if Greek wine is used, it should not be a retsina)
3 onions
½ tsp cinnamon

Dice the precooked pork into pieces about ¾ inch square. Peel and chop the onions. Put the white wine and vinegar into a frying pan, and simmer the pork and onions in this for about 15 minutes. Add the spices and sugar, and simmer for a further 5 minutes, stirring gently. Add salt to taste.

c. 1380

GOLDEN APPLES [for 4 persons]

(Powme dorys.)

This would originally have been cooked on a spit or perhaps skewers; in a modern kitchen it is much simpler to grill it, using kebab skewers.

1½ lb minced raw pork
1 oz large raisins
1 tsp chopped parsley

4 eggs
pinch ground saffron
2 tsp flour

Mix the raw pork, saffron and the raisins, and form into balls, pressing them firmly together. Separate the egg yolks from the whites. Dip the meat balls into the egg whites until thoroughly coated. Fill a small sauce-pan about three-quarters full with salted water, and bring to the boil. Dip the meat balls in gently with a spoon, and cook for about 3–5 minutes. Preheat the grill. Blend the flour, parsley and egg yolks. Drain the meat balls carefully, put on skewers, and put under the grill to brown, turning once. Remove from grill and glaze with egg yolk. Brown lightly under grill. Remove again, turn and glaze other side. Brown this lightly. Withdraw skewers and serve.

c. 1380

CHARLET [for 4 persons]

1 lb diced cold pork	*¼ pt milk*
4 eggs	*pinch saffron*

Put cold pork into frying pan. Break eggs over this and stir, but *not* over heat. Stir in the milk and saffron, and bring slowly to the boil. With-draw from heat as soon as the eggs are cooked. Season with salt and serve.

c. 1380

HANONEY [for 2 persons]

This is one of the earliest references to the use of butter for frying.

4 eggs	*1 onion*
1 oz butter	

Chop onion and fry in butter, but do not allow to brown. Separate egg yolks and whites. Strain both through sieve and mix. Add this to fried onion, and stir gently until cooked.

c. 1430–50

EGREDOUNCY [for 4 persons]

The name might mean sweet and sour (sour = *aigre*, sweet = *douce*)

1 lb cold pork	*1½ pt pork or chicken stock*
2 onions	*3 tbs vinegar*
2 tbs breadcrumbs	*2 tsp chopped parsley*
1 tsp chopped sage	*½ tsp pepper*
1 tsp cinnamon	*pinch saffron*

Mince the cold pork. Simmer the peeled and sliced onions in the stock for 10 minutes. Then add the saffron, parsley, sage and minced pork, and thicken with breadcrumbs. Continue to simmer for a further 10 minutes. Add pepper, cinnamon and vinegar and bring to the boil again. The consistency should be on the liquid side rather than too thick, so do not allow to boil for more than a minute or two.

c. 1380

FILLETS IN GALANTINE [for 4 persons]

4 pieces pork fillet (about 1¾ lb)	*¾ pt beef stock*
1 tbs vinegar	*3 crushed cloves*
2 slices brown bread	*½ tsp mace*

For galantine (in a medieval kitchen, this was probably kept made up)

2 breadcrusts	*4 tbs wine vinegar*
½ tsp ground ginger	*½ tsp cinnamon*

Prepare the galantine by soaking the breadcrusts in 3 tbs vinegar. Pound and sieve this, adding the rest of the vinegar, the ginger and the cinnamon; the result should be a smooth thick sauce.

Tie and roast the fillets until almost cooked (30–40 minutes, Regulo Mark 6, 400°). Soak the bread in ¼ pt stock and the vinegar. When the fillets are ready, untie them and put in a large saucepan with the rest of the stock and the bread, adding any liquid from roasting. Bring this to the boil, add the spices and the galantine, and simmer gently for 10 minutes.

c. 1420

TART ON EMBER DAY [for 4 persons]

Ember Days were the seasonal three days of fasting which occurred four times a year, after the first Sunday in Lent, Whitsun, Holy Rood Day (14 September) and St Lucy's Day (13 December).

½ lb onions	*1 oz sugar*
½ tsp sage	*1 oz raisins*
1 tsp chopped parsley	*1 tsp cinnamon*
½ lb cream cheese	*2 pieces stem ginger*
3 eggs	*pastry for flan case*
2 oz butter	

Chop the stem ginger as finely as possible. Parboil the onions, sage and parsley in 1½ pts water in a medium saucepan. Drain and chop finely. Mix this with the cheese and the remaining ingredients. Line flan case with pastry, and fill with mixture. Bake in a medium oven (Regulo Mark 4, 340°) for 20 minutes.

c. 1420

A DISH OF LIVER [for 4 persons]

½ *lb liver*   *3 hard-boiled eggs*
2½ *glasses sweet white wine*   *2 onions*

Slice onions and fry lightly in oil. Drain. Chop liver and hard-boiled eggs, add sweet white wine, and put in liquidizer. Reduce to smooth consistency, add onions and fry in oil until mixture is just beginning to dry.

This should be served as a side dish with other meat and vegetables.

German, *c.* 1375–1400

SAUCE FOR ROAST MUTTON

½ *lb onions*   *4 tsp chopped parsley*
3 tbs vinegar   *2 pieces stem ginger, chopped finely*
½ *tsp salt*

Peel and slice onions and boil with parsley in a medium saucepan in 1 pt water. When soft, drain and mince. Mix the vinegar, salt and chopped ginger, and add to the onions and parsley.

c. 1430

TANSY [for 2 persons]

4 eggs   *tsp finely ground tansy*
lard

Separate egg whites and yolks, and put through sieve. Mix together and add tansy. Fry in lard, without stirring, in a 7-inch pan; when thoroughly set, turn in one piece, and cook other side. The result should be a kind of flat egg sponge, not an omelette.

c. 1430–50

JUSSELL [for 4 persons]

4 eggs   *8 oz breadcrumbs*
pinch saffron   *tsp ground sage*
1 pt chicken stock

Mix eggs and breadcrumbs, beating well. Stir in sage, saffron and chicken stock and beat until smooth. Put in a medium saucepan, bring to the boil, and simmer for 5–7 minutes.

c. 1480

SLIT SOPS [for 4 persons]

4 leeks   *1 glass wine*
3 tbs oil   *tsp salt*
4 slices brown bread

Wash leeks and take off outer leaves; cut off tops to leave only whites, and trim bottoms. Split each leek down the middle. Put the wine, oil and salt in a large saucepan, and simmer the leeks in this for 15 minutes, covering the pan. Toast the bread and trim off the crusts. When cooked, pour the stock over the toast and place the leeks on top.

c. 1380

A DISH OF BEANS

1 lb runner beans   *½ pt brown ale*
1 oz white breadcrumbs   *3 tbs vinegar*
½ tsp pepper   *pinch saffron*
1½ tsp ground caraway seed

Boil the beans in ½ pt water in a medium saucepan until soft. Mix the remaining ingredients together, and put in a small saucepan, bringing just to the boil. Drain the beans, and pour the sauce over them before serving.

German, *c.* 1375–1400

TURNESOLE [for 4 persons]

So called from its colour: turnsole was a kind of violet dye.

½ lb blackberries   *4 oz ground almonds*
½ pt milk   *3 glasses sweet white wine*
1 oz rice flour or ground rice   *2 oz sugar*

Soak the blackberries in half the wine for an hour. Stir the almonds into the milk, add the remaining wine and bring to the boil. Add the sugar, and thicken with the rice flour. Add the blackberries and the juice, stir well, bring just to the boil, and serve.

c. 1420

DOUCETTES [for 4 persons]

This is one of the few recipes that specifically require an oven, apart from pies and pasties which were made by bakers and do not appear in the early cookery books.

¼ pt double cream	3 egg yolks
1 tbs milk	4 oz icing sugar
pinch saffron	pastry for pie cases

Bake the empty pie cases until just brown; fill with baking beans on silver foil to prevent them from rising. Warm the milk and stir in the saffron. Strain the cream and the yolks of egg through a sieve and add the icing sugar and milk. Beat well. Make sure that the custard is smooth. Fill the pie cases with the mixture, and bake until it rises (5–10 minutes at Regulo Mark 5, 360°).

c. 1480

CHERRIES   [for 4 persons]

1 lb cherries	tsp cinnamon
1 tbs lard	3 egg yolks
1 tbs rice flour	pinch saffron
2 tsp sugar	1 tbs vinegar

Stone the cherries. Put about a dozen on one side. Purée the remainder. Add lard and rice flour, and put in a medium saucepan. Thicken over a low flame, adding more rice flour if necessary. Stir in sugar, vinegar and cinnamon; add yolks of egg and stir until smooth. Colour with saffron and serve with the remaining whole cherries planted round the edge.

c. 1420

CAWDEL FERRY   [for 4 persons]

8 oz white breadcrumbs	1 pt white wine
8 oz sugar	4 egg yolks
½ tsp salt	tsp ground ginger
2 tbs sugar, for dusting	pinch saffron

Stir breadcrumbs and saffron into wine, and mix with sugar. Put in a medium saucepan and bring to the boil. Simmer for 10 minutes. Add egg yolks and salt, and stir until egg is completely absorbed. Powder with ginger and sugar before serving.

c. 1420

RAPEYE   [for 4 persons]

½ lb figs	½ oz rice flour
4 oz raisins	¼ pt sweet white wine
pepper and salt	½ tsp cinnamon

Scald the figs and raisins in wine in a shallow pan to soften them. Put them and the wine aside to cool; when cool put in liquidizer and blend. Add spices, and return to the saucepan. Bring almost to boil, thicken with rice flour and add salt to taste before serving.

c. 1430

CABBAGE [for 4 persons]

1 cabbage
½ lb bone marrow
pinch powdered saffron

¾ pt beef or mutton stock
2 oz brown breadcrumbs
¼ tsp salt

Clean, wash and parboil the cabbage in 1½ pts water in a medium saucepan. Press out the water on a chopping board, and put back in the saucepan with the beef stock and bone marrow. Bring to the boil and simmer for about 5 minutes. Add the breadcrumbs, saffron and salt, and simmer for a further 2 minutes.

c. 1430

PEARS EN COMPOTE [for 6 persons]

6 dessert pears
8 oz white sugar
4 oz sliced dates

½ pt red wine
2 tsp cinnamon
salt

Heat the wine, sugar and cinnamon over a low flame in a medium saucepan. Do not allow to boil. Peel, core and slice the pears, and add these and the dates to the syrup. Allow to boil, adding a little salt. When the pears are soft, pour the contents of the saucepan into a wooden bowl and serve.

c. 1430

APPLEMOY

1½ lb dessert apples
½ pt milk
pinch saffron
salt

2 oz almonds
½ oz ground rice
2 tbs honey

Peel and core apples; stew in medium saucepan with saffron in ¾ pt water until soft. Add almonds to milk, warm gently and stir in honey and ground rice. Add puréed apples to this, and season with salt. Adjust thickness – it should be very thick – by adding more ground rice if necessary.

c. 1380

A DISH OF PEARS   [for 4 persons]

4 dessert pears	*¾ tsp aniseed*
3 eggs	*brown bread*
2 green cooking apples	*butter*
¼ tsp pepper	

Bake the apples and pears in the oven until just soft (20–25 minutes at
Regulo Mark 4, 340° . Peel, core and dice. Add pepper, aniseed and two
eggs, and beat together. Cut slices of brown bread as thin as possible.
Fill each pair of slices with the mixture. Beat the remaining egg and use
to glaze the bread. Fry in butter until brown, turning once.

German c. 1375–1400

FIG SOUP   [for 4 persons]

(*Fygge to potage.*)

½ lb dessert figs	
(Fresh or dessert figs will do equally well, but slightly more honey will be needed with fresh figs)	*1 pt water*
	tsp powdered ginger
2 oz raisins	*¼ pt wine*
3 oz ground almonds	*2 tbs honey*

Blend the ground almonds as smoothly as possible with the water and
wine. Quarter the figs. Bring the liquid to the boil in a medium saucepan, add the figs, raisins, ginger and honey. Simmer gently for 15–20
minutes.

c. 1420

POKEROUNCE   [for 4 persons]

4 tbs honey	*4 oz pine-kernels*
½ tsp cinnamon	*white bread*
¼ tsp ginger	

Put honey in a small frying pan and bring to boil. Simmer for 2 minutes.
Remove from heat and stir in ginger and cinnamon. Toast bread and
spread the mixture on this. Sprinkle with pine-kernels and serve.

c. 1420

Figure 6 A feast at Ferrara in the mid sixteenth-century, from Messi Sbugo's *Conviti* (1555).

By the middle of the fifteenth century, great feasts had acquired a very special place in court life, as the chief means of displaying royal pomp and splendour and as a weapon in diplomacy. Ambassadors and subjects alike were overawed by means of massive displays of extravagance, often allied with theatrical interludes with a pointed political message. The most celebrated example of this kind of banquet-festival was the famous 'Oath of the Pheasant' at Lille in 1454, when Philip the Good took a vow to go on crusade against the Turks, in itself the culmination of a series of magnificent feasts given by his nobles. The details read like some strange dream, as though Hieronymus Bosch had been the master of ceremonies:

Even from across the sea people came to view the gorgeous spectacle. Besides the guests, a great number of noble spectators were present at the feast, disguised for the most part. First every one walked about to admire the fixed show-pieces; later came the 'entremets', that is to say, representations of 'personnages' and tableaux vivants. Olivier [de la Marche, who recorded the event] himself played the important part of Holy Church, making his appearance in a tower on the back of an elephant, led by a gigantic Turk. The tables were loaded with the most extravagant decorations. There were a rigged and ornamented carack, a meadow surrounded by trees with a fountain, rocks, and a statue of St Andrew, the castle of Lusignan with the fairy Melusine, a bird-shooting scene near a windmill, a wood in which wild beasts walked about, and, lastly, a church with an organ and singers, whose songs alternated with the music of the orchestra of twenty-eight persons, which was placed in a pie.

Great painters were often employed on such occasions, and immense ingenuity went into the contriving of mechanical tricks and illusions. Sometimes these got out of hand, as at the Field of the Cloth of Gold in 1515, when the dragon filled with fireworks went off too soon, and floated through the air during Mass, to the astonishment of the congregation. And if the cook's skill was admired at all, it was for his engineering skill in concealing the orchestra in a pie, or for some overblown version of the old-fashioned 'subtlety'. On the whole, however, realism was the keynote, and the subtleties, with their brief but pointed mottoes or 'reasons', were replaced by living actors. Olivier de la Marche's part at Lille, representing the hoped-for triumph over the infidel in the course of which he sang a long elegy, would have been summed up a century before on a much more modest scale by a figure made by the cook. So it is scarcely surprising that all the splendours of the Burgundian court in the first half of the fifteenth century have left no mark on the history of cookery, and that the chroniclers tended to describe the table decorations rather than the menu. Written menus may have existed, since they were reputedly introduced by Queen Isabeau at the French court in the 1380s, but they competed unsuccessfully for attention with the orchestras, mimes and allegories.

The Burgundian ideas on festivals were in many ways an exaggerated development of what had been presented in Italy in the previous century. The Italian feasts themselves continued on as lavish a scale as ever: the Bentivoglio family at Bologna, the Sforzas at Milan, the Medici at Florence all vied with each other in magnificence, both at table and in secular 'triumphs', based on the rejoicings, in classical times, of a grateful Rome when one of their generals returned victorious. And it was from Rome itself that the next revival of the cook's art was to come.

The popes of the Renaissance were as much princes as prelates, and it was from the inmost circle of the papal court that the first printed cookery book derived. Bartolomeo Sacchi of Cremona, known as Platina, was one of the leading lights of an institution called the Academy. This club for lovers of classical antiquity was founded by Giulio Pomponio Leto about 1460; its members used Greek names and studied ancient manners, thought and history. Although many leading figures in Rome belonged to it, in the intrigues of the day such pagan pursuits could bring a charge of heresy; and Platina was indeed imprisoned under Pope Paul II, partly for alleged complicity in a plot against the pope, partly for his suspect interest in Greek learning. But he was released in 1470, just before his work on cookery appeared.

De Honesta Voluptate he called it, *On Lawful Pleasure*, with half an eye on the officials who had taken such a poor view of his thinking a little earlier, and might now condemn him as a lover of fleshly delights; and he is careful to explain that he is interested only in a legitimate, moderate appetite. Much of the book, however, betrays both his and Rome's enjoyment of good food. He dedicates the book to the Cardinal of St Clement's, saying, 'Do not despise these rustic exercises of mine, which I wrote in my Tuscan retreat at the home of Francesco Gonzaga'. And there are a number of references to other friends, sometimes under the Greek names by which they were known at the Academy. It is the first systematic cookery book since Apicius, divided into eight headings: fruit and seasonings, nuts and herbs, salads and meats (including three recipes for a modern pâté), two sections on poultry, prepared dishes, sweets and, finally, eggs and frying. Quantities are often given, as well as the number of people that they will be sufficient for. It is both a practical and a personal book, written in purest Renaissance Latin; surely one of the most elegantly composed of cookery books. There are a number of Spanish recipes, reflected the growing Spanish influence at the papal court as well as the Spanish domination of southern Italy. At the end of one of these, for *mirrauste*, he notes: 'I cannot remember eating anything more delicious with my friend Valdischara.' And of a Catalonian *blanc manger* he says: 'Our friend Galbes often used to invite Rizo and myself to share this dish; and Tridentus was there too, who declared that he had never eaten anything more pleasing.' A few recipes have classical names, though they are not the same as the classical originals, and some medieval dishes survive, such as dariols. More modern are his references to *œufs florentine, ova fricta florentinorum more*, though these are not what we would understand by the title (p. 20), and to caviar, 'which the Greeks eat most avidly'.

Platina's work proved very popular, and it was reprinted a number of times in northern Italy before the end of the century; French and German translations were published in 1505 and 1530, and its influence was probably greater than that of any other cookery book up to this period. Platina himself was appointed Vatican librarian by Sixtus IV, though this was in recognition of his historical work on the lives of the first hundred popes rather than his gastronomic researches. The popes of the late Renaissance continued to show a great interest in the pleasures of the table, and a succession of works by papal cooks dominated the literature on cookery for the next century. Of these books, the most important

were those by Giovane, Spanish chef to Clement VII, and by
Bartolomeo Scappi. The chief interest in Giovane's book is the
repeated Spanish influence which we have already noted in
Platina. *Mirrauste* and *pavon* both figure in the work, the latter as
pavonazo; the recipe is given on p. 118. Giovane, however, is by
no means exclusively Spanish in his choice of dishes; he offers a
variety of pasta, including macaroni in Sicilian and Roman style,
and ravioli. These recipes are probably much older than their first
appearance in print; the fourteenth-century cookery books show
that pasta was already established then, and the varieties which
do not appear there are more likely to have gone unrecorded than
to have been the invention of chefs. Among other traditional 'folk'
recipes is *torta bolognese*.

Bartolomeo Scappi's book, published in 1570, is about the size
of Mrs Beeton, and is one of the earliest attempts at a comprehensive guide to cooking. Scappi was personal cook to Pope Pius V,
and the book is designed for princely households. The introduction
consists of a dialogue between the author and an apprentice on the
principles of buying and preserving food; there is a section of
menus, and a concluding chapter on diet for invalids. Part of the
length of the book is due to Scappi's love of longwinded instructions, which he often repeats unnecessarily. In the section on
meat, beef and veal predominate and mutton is not used, while
tagliatelle and *gnocchi* appear among the pasta. Other items included
are a list of equipment for a travelling kitchen, and a very detailed
set of illustrations shows us the furniture and utensils of a sixteenth-
century kitchen.

Other books reveal the increasing interest both in domestic
economy and in special aspects of serving. Domenico Romoli's
work entitled *The whole doctrine of the office of chef* appeared in
1560, and lays great stress on household management; indeed the
Italian word *scalco* is probably better translated steward, though
an English steward would not have had the same knowledge of
the kitchen and its workings. Romoli begins with a list of household
officers, and continues with a lengthy recital both of the seasons
for various meats, fish and vegetables, and of the menus appropriate to the time of year. Two sections of recipes are followed by
another two chapters in which the medical side of cookery re-

appears, analysing the properties of various meats according to the medieval theory of the four elements which we outlined earlier. The book is rounded off with more medical lore in the form of rules for health.

Figure 7 Cesare Evitascandalo.

Cesare Evitascandalo's book of 1598 begins with a similar introduction to Romoli's, but is more lively. The chief problem in hiring a cook is to find one who is both clean and honest; he should not be given the remains of lard, wood and oil as perquisites, because this will only make him extravagant. The *scalco* is expected to make all the necessary decisions about the running of the kitchen; if he merely lets the cook decide which dishes are to be served, he is no true *scalco* but a mere carrier of dishes. Properly fulfilled, the office of *scalco* is the greatest responsibility in the court, or so Evitascandalo, himself a holder of the office, claims. Two other officers are under his command besides the cook: the *credentiero*, or waiter in charge of the buffet, from which every other course is served and on which spices and sauces are kept, so that it was as important as the kitchen as a source of food at a feast; and the *spenditore* or bursar. The *scalco* must also know how to place guests at the table, and be conversant with all the rules of etiquette.

The planning of menus was an equally demanding operation. No two similar dishes are to follow each other, and Evitascandalo provides long lists of possible combinations. He gives a menu for a state dinner in six services: each course consists of eleven dishes each with four condiments, beginning with a service from the buffet, then three services from the kitchen, and ending with two from the buffet. The first and last two courses are, of course, all cold dishes, an *hors d'œuvre* and two courses of sweets. And even this elaborate offering is described as 'a mediocre meal' which could be improved by the use of more expensive materials. Of the eleven dishes in each course, the guests would naturally have tasted only one or two. Evitascandalo pours scorn on the way in which meals are served in Germany. Here round or square individual tables are used, instead of the oblong tables arranged together in an open-sided square in Italy. Each course consists of one dish, of which all the guests partake. As a result the Germans often spend four hours or more over a meal, particularly if the menu has seventeen courses, as in the example which Evitascandalo gives.

A certain degree of waste was regarded as obligatory in a noble household, as appears from the menu for a day when the head of the household was to dine alone. This consisted of two roast and two boiled meats, with five other items in the first course and four items in the dessert. The reason for this extensive choice is not that the lord will have all his family with him, or that the left-overs will be used to feed the rest of the household, but simply that this is the style that is expected of him; anything else would not be 'decent and honourable'.

A suitable display was also one of the main preoccupations of Vittorio Lancellotti's *Scalco Practico* of 1627. Here the service from the buffet has become a formal framework to the meal, providing an *hors d'œuvre* (often laid out before the guests took their places) and a dessert only; but the buffet is also used for an exhibition of pastries and confectioneries, the medieval subtlety restored to its former glory. Even an *al fresco* supper given by Cardinal Aldobrandini in 1626 had to have such a display mounted indoors as a postscript to the proceedings. At a dinner given by the same cardinal for the prince of Savoy, there was no room on the groaning buffet for pastries and showpieces, which had to be omitted. The ultimate in the meal as a ceremonial occasion, with its own special heraldry, is a little watercolour which shows ex-Queen Christina of Sweden dining with Pope Clement IX in 1658, where the two solitary figures on the dais look as symbolic and statuesque as the sugar confections that hedge them in.

Carving, too, played its part in the ceremonial aspect of dining to a greater extent than ever before. Vincenzo Cervio's treatise *Il Trinciante* (*The Carver*) not only shows how to carve meat and poultry, but also includes in its detailed plates a series of geometrical fantasies which turn out to be peeled fruit. Carving was usually done *in alto*, in the air, with the object to be carved impaled on the fork. The warning of a later German writer was probably all too necessary at state occasions, where the carver was apt to become self-important or nervous: 'In all his carving he should avoid violent movement and unnecessary foolish ceremonies, which only prolong the carving, and he should see that he is not frightened and does not disgrace himself by trembling, whether in his body or hands.' If he was trying to remember Cervio's precise instructions as to the exact placing of the knife for each cut, the appropriate parts to be carved for each person, and the carefully ritualized movements, he might well have contracted stage fright.

Nor was it always the carver who might forget the preference of a guest or host. There is a story that Pope Julius III, enraged by his kitchen's failure to serve up a peacock, was reproved by one of his cardinals for his anger over so trifling a matter. At which the pontiff rounded on him with the comment that God himself had been vexed by a missing apple. If, however, it was a cook like Antonio Frugoli who made the omission, it might well have been because he disapproved of his patron's choice. In his *Pratica e Scalcaria*, he has some sharp words to say apropos of eating ostrich:

The ostrich is of the worst possible quality, even worse than the crane which we have just discussed; because this creature is so hot by nature that it digests iron, and its meat should not be eaten because it is of such poor quality, and its body is so large that its feathers cannot support it in flight, because they are very pliable, although it runs very swiftly, and has cloven feet like quadrupeds, and has various other qualities which I omit for the moment, merely noting that when Antonius Elagabalus was emperor, among various dishes of many meats which appeared at his table, he once had bought six hundred ostrich heads, and the brains alone were eaten, although I believe that he did it more out of curiosity than because it contained any goodness, or because the brains of birds exceed in goodness those of animals, and are a little better, as I have said.

It may be that curiosities are pleasing to most of the guests, providing that they are meats of some usefulness and not mere whims, and good stewards must take particular care not to serve whimsical dishes, but indeed ones of some usefulness and goodness; but as to the ways of cooking the flesh of the said ostrich, although it is not difficult, I leave it aside in any case, because they are not often found in these parts, because such creatures live in deserts.

When we turn to French cookery, we find a more down-to-earth view of the cook's art. The early French printed cookery books are surprisingly conservative. The medieval tradition predominated until the early seventeenth century, by which time Italian influences in painting and literature were firmly established in France, and indeed beginning to decline again; but of Italian cookery there is very little trace. *The Livre Fort Excellent de Cuisine*, which appeared at Lyon in 1542, the *Grand Cuisinier* (Paris, about 1566), and Pierre Pidoux's *Fleur de Toute Cuysine* of 1543 contain mostly recipes which would have been familiar to Taillevent (whose own work appeared in print in 1490) or to the author of *The Parisian Housekeeper*. Such novelties as there are seem to be native inventions, not always successful: the instructions for cooking cormorant, according to one bold experimenter, are to be avoided at all costs! Rabelais, describing the feasts of his heroes Gargantua and Pantagruel, offers a menu that is still medieval, although he himself had travelled in Italy. The favourite dishes that he parades before us are native French country cooking; indeed, for a character whose name has become a byword for gluttony, Gargantua's meals are surprisingly unadventurous. But then most of Rabelais's satire looks backwards to traditional abuses and ancient errors, and this antiquated diet accords well with the medieval ways of the monks, clergy and lawyers which he attacks.

Novelties did sometimes appear, however, in the shape of welcome additions to the menu throughout Europe. Among them at this period were the turkey, the potato and a number of fruits. Turkeys were first seen by the Spanish conquistadors in the 1520s, and were imported to Europe from the West Indies by 1530. They quickly became popular; by 1541, they appear in an English document which forbids prelates to be served with more than one of the 'greater fowles' in a dish at dinner, and by the 1570s Thomas Tusser describes them as part of 'Christmas husbandlie fare', the farmer's Christmas dinner. Potatoes, which the Spaniards found rather later when they reached Peru, were imported to Spain in the 1560s, and reached Italy and Belgium from there. They were also brought independently by Sir Walter Raleigh to Ireland in 1586. The early Spanish and Italian plants seem to have been a sweeter variety than Raleigh's; to judge by the recipes given for cooking them, which use wine and sugar, they were considerably different from our modern plants. Oranges, although known as a rarity in the Middle Ages, were grown in Europe on a large scale only after the beginning of the sixteenth century when trees were imported from the Levant. The most exotic item of all was the pineapple, which came from Brazil in 1555, but it was not successfully cultivated in Europe until the end of the following century. Its rarity and decorative shape led the cabinetmakers of the late seventeenth and early eighteenth century to use it as a pattern for knobs and finials, though they had probably never seen the real fruit, let alone tasted one.

The French religious wars of the end of the sixteenth century were no fit time for innovations in cookery; but in the early seventeenth century Catherine de' Medici, mother of Louis XIII and real ruler of France during his youth, brought her Italian entourage to France. Tradition has it that her Florentine cooks laid the foundations of French cooking. However, since there is no trace of any particularly distinguished cooking from Florence at the period, compared with Rome or Venice, the cooks are much more likely to have drawn on the Roman tradition we have already outlined. Another innovation from Italy, this time from Venice, was the use of the fork, which reached France at about the same period. As the English traveller Thomas Coryat records:

I observed a custome in all those Italian Cities and townes through the which I passed, that is not used in any other country that I saw in my travels, neither doe I thinke that any other nation of Christendome doth use it, but only Italy. The Italian and also most strangers that are commorant in Italy, doe alwaies at their meales use a little forke when they cut their meat. For while with their knife which they hold in one hand they cut the meate out of the dish, they fasten their forke which they hold in their other hand upon the same dish, so that whatsoever he be that sitting in the company of any others at meale, shoulde un-advisedly touch the dishe of meate with his fingers from which all at table doe cut, he will give occasion of offence unto the company, as having transgressed the lawes of good manners, in so much that for his error, he shall be at the least brow-beaten, if not reprehended in wordes. This forme of feeding I understand is generally used in all places of Italy, their forkes being for the most part made of yron or steele, and some of silver, but those are used only by Gentlemen. The reason of this their curiosity is, because the Italian cannot by any means indure to have his dish touched with fingers, seeing all men's fingers are not alike cleane. Hereupon I myselfe thought good to imitate the Italian fashion by this forked cutting of meate, not only while I was in Italy, but also in Germany, and oftentimes in England since I came home.

This new implement abolished with one swift stab the medieval pottages, stews and purées, and reduced the importance of elaborate spicery, since the ingredients could now be cooked in a way that preserved their own particular flavour. One reason suggested for the new fashion of feeding with forks is that the huge ruffs of the period made it more difficult to eat cleanly with the fingers without soiling the ruff. At all events, the medieval messes disappear, and simplicity and subtlety are the new keynotes. (Incidentally, a mess was originally no more than a dish of food; we use the word to mean a muddle or state of confusion because that was how old-fashioned cookery appeared to more sophisticated eyes.)

The great age of French cooking begins under Louis XIV, and

here one figure stands out: François Pierre de la Varenne. La
Varenne, so the story goes, was a scullion in the kitchen of the
duchess of Bar, sister of Henri IV, and was entrusted by the latter
with some delicate negotiations over a girl; his skill in such matters
was so well rewarded that the duchess said to him in later years:
'You earned more by acting as porter for my brother's birds than
you did for turning mine on a spit.' His two books, *Le Vray
Cuisiniesr* and *Le Pastissier François*, published in the 1650s, are the
basis of modern European *haute cuisine*. The thick stews and highly
spiced vegetables, which we can paradoxically appreciate better
for knowing what their ingredients are like when plainly cooked,
were banished, and in their place came more elegant preparations
based on sauces made with flour accompanying a main ingredient
which had not been hacked, chopped or otherwise disguised.
Spices were also treated with suspicion, and only vinegar was
allowed in any quantity, to provide piquancy where earlier cooks
had all too often merely overpowered with pungent flavours. He
introduces truffles in a new way, using them as a flavouring rather
than a pickle, which had been the old method; and he offers
a much better organized system of using stock, beginning with a
basic meat stock of beef, mutton and chicken seasoned with a
bundle of parsley, shallots, thyme and a few cloves. The famous
sauce Robert appears for the first time. Among vegetables he uses
the globe artichoke extensively, and in general vegetables are
carefully treated in order to bring out their flavour. But even as
great a chef as this has his extravagances – sausages made of
partridges' brains are hardly a simple dish – and his rivals had some
sharp words to say about him. 'L.S.R.', whose *Art de bien traiter*
appeared at much the same time, and is if anything even plainer
than La Varenne, exaggerates the case against him in his preface:

I fully believe that there are none of those absurdities and disgusting
lessons here which the Sieur de Varenne dares to offer and champion,
with which he has for a long time ensnared and lulled the stupid and
ignorant people, passing off his productions as so many infallible truths
. . . Do you not shudder at the idea of soup of teal with hypocras, of
larks in sweet sauce ? . . . and an infinity of other knaveries which one
would suffer more willingly among the Arabs and the savages than in a
pure climate like our own.

La Varenne's other book, *Le Pastissier François* (Plate 14), is notorious for being a great rarity among cookery books; in the edition printed by the famous Dutch firm of Elsevier, it is sought after by lovers of fine printing and of cookery alike. The pastry-cook's art was well established as a separate branch of cooking. As early as 1292, Paris city records show sixty-eight pastrycooks working in the capital, including various specialists: seven made only crêpes, and twenty-six were makers of sweet pastry. But there had been no guide to their art until La Varenne's work, and although it has little that recommends itself in a modern kitchen, being mostly a matter of large quantities and a strong right arm, it is entertaining to see how complex some of the procedures are. The most easily accessible section is that on eggs, which includes ten ways of poaching them and twenty-two ways of making an omelette, a dish which had evidently been much explored since Taillevent's recipe 250 years earlier. La Varenne offers a stuffed omelette containing sweet herbs, yolks of hard-boiled eggs and half-cooked chopped mushrooms which is excellent. His scrambled egg is less palatable, using orange juice and a teaspoon of verjuice per egg.

La Varenne had a number of other imitators and competitors beside 'L.S.R.'. Pierre de Lune's *Le Nouveau Cuisinier* of 1660 is arranged according to the season, and reflects the food of a noble household rather than La Varenne's more general approach; de Lune had been cook to the Duc de Rohan, one of France's greatest nobles. His *farine frite* is an early version of a basic *roux*:

Fry flour in lard, stirring with a silver spoon until brown. Add stock, a bouquet of herbs, lemon and a piece of sliced beef. The bouquet should consist of a strip of fat, a spring onion, thyme, parsley, cloves and chervil, tied with a piece of string.

Just as the new fashions in cookery had been a butt for the satirists of ancient Rome, so the French writers who consciously set out to imitate Horace and Juvenal took the gourmet or would-be gourmet as a target. Boileau describes a dinner-party very much on the Horatian model, culminating in a roast – of sorts:

Surrounded by six hectic chickens, lo, a hare!
Atop of all, three home-bred rabbits rise in air,

Who from their tender youth in Paris had been bred,
And gave forth fumes of cabbage on which they'd fed.
Around this heaped up mass of dainties was a string
Of dried up flattened larks all marshalled in a ring.
Then, ranged about the dish, six pigeons hold their post,
Defending with their squalid skeletons the roast.
Two salad bowls appear beside the famous mess,
One of yellow purslain and one of faded cress,
Of which the rancid oil from far offends our noses
And swims upon a flood of vinegar of roses.

But both Boileau's raillery and another episode of the period
betray a seriousness about food which the French have never quite
contrived to lose and the English have never quite appreciated.
Mme de Sévigné tells the other story in one of her letters, tragi-
comedy against Boileau's farce, about the death of the *maître
d'hôtel* of the Prince de Condé:

Moreuil has just told me what happened at Chantilly, apropos of Vatel.
Here is the full story. The king arrived on the Thursday evening; the
promenade, the light supper in a spot carpeted with jonquils, everything was as perfect as one could wish. Supper was served, and there
were a few tables at which the roast was lacking, because of a number
of diners who had not been in the least expected. This obsessed Vatel;
he said several times: 'I am dishonoured, I cannot bear such a disgrace.'
He said to Gourville: 'My head is spinning, I haven't slept for twelve
nights: help me to give orders.' Gourville assisted him as far as he
could. The roast, which had been lacking, not for the king's table, but
for the twenty-fifth table (in order of precedence) preyed on his mind.
Gourville told the Prince de Condé. The prince went to Vatel's room
and told him: 'Vatel, everything is all right; nothing could have been so
excellent as the king's supper.' 'My lord, I'm overwhelmed by your
kindness; I know that there was no roast at two tables.' 'Not at all,'
said the prince, 'don't worry, everything is going well.' At midnight the
fireworks failed because they were hidden in mist; they had cost sixteen
thousand francs. At four in the morning, Vatel went on his rounds and
found everyone asleep; he met a little merchant who had brought just
a couple of baskets of fresh fish, and asked him: 'Is that all?' 'Yes, sir,'
he answered, not knowing that Vatel had sent to all the seaports for
supplies. Vatel waited a little longer; the other merchants did not
arrive; he grew hysterical, and thought that no more fresh fish would

arrive. He found Gourville and told him: 'I shall never survive this disgrace.' Gourville laughed at him. Vatel went up to his room, placed his sword against the door, and ran it through his body; but he only succeeded at the third blow, for he gave himself two other wounds which were not fatal, before he fell dead. The fresh fish, however, came in from every side; Vatel was wanted to distribute it, they went to his room, knocked, broke down the door, and found him in a pool of blood. The prince was in despair when he heard; the duke wept; his whole journey to Burgundy depended on Vatel. The prince told the king, full of sorrow; people said he had done it because he was so sensitive about his honour; he was much praised, praised and censured for his courage. Gourville tried to make good the loss of Vatel; it *was* made good; dinner was excellent, supper, promenades, games, hunting, everything was scented with jonquils, everything was under a magic spell.

Across the Rhine, the Germans took their eating quite as seriously as the French. The Lutheran clergy, according to Catholic propaganda, were reputed to be great trenchermen, inheriting the bad name of the medieval monks. In both cases, there was probably little justification for the libel. But German food seems to have consisted more in quantity than in refined cookery, since only a handful of printed cookery books, none of them particularly distinguished, have survived. The earliest, a little work of forty-two pages called *Kuchenmeisterei* (*The Cook's Art*) appeared in 1495. As the sixteenth century progressed, the collections grew in size; *Koch- und Kellermeisterei* (*The Art of Cooking and Brewing*) ran through a number of editions, each slightly larger than its predecessor. It contains fairly simple recipes, often transcriptions of medieval ones; a particular feature is the use of fruit to accompany meat. There is even an early form of *muesli*, in which roasted or boiled grapes, apples and pears are mixed with oatmeal and sugar and boiled. The later, larger books draw heavily on Italian sources: Harssdorffer's *Trincirbuch* (*Carving Book*) of 1665 uses the same illustrations as Cervio's work published in Venice in 1581, and Max Rumpolt's enormous cookery book of 1604 owes much to Scappi and earlier writers who had worked out a classified division of kinds of food. It is an engaging book, with delightful woodcuts which would deter anyone from eating the animals or birds illustrated; who would want to check

Om wilden Pferdt kan man zurichten in einem schwartzen.
Pfeffer / Vnd wenn du es braten wilt / so saltz es wol / denn es
ist ein süsses Fleisch / kanst den Braten auch mit Knobloch zurichten. Wenn man es will im Pfeffer kochen / so setzt mans zu
mit Wasser / wol gesaltzen / wenns wol gesaltzen / so zeucht man
es auff ein Bret auß / vnd letzts kalt werden / Mach ein guten Vngerischen
Pfeffer mit Hennenschweiß / der fein säurlich ist / Vnd wenn der Pfeffer zu-
gerichtist / so thu das Fleisch darein / so wirdt es gut vnd lieblich. Du
kanst auch die Geil / wie von einem Eynheimischen Pferdt
zurichten / wie vorhin vermeldt ist von
der Böck Geil.

Figure 8   Instructions for cooking a wild horse from Max Rumpolt's cookery book.

the wild horse (above) in mid-career to bring him to the table?
Rumpolt does, it is true, extend the list of edible creatures to the
utmost limits; his enormously long title-page could be reduced
to 'How to cook everything' without doing him an injustice.
And he offers menus for everybody as well, from prelates and
princes down to citizens and peasants. Rumpolt also lays particular stress on looking after the servants at a banquet; when the
guests have departed, the steward is to lay a clean cloth, and see
that they are decently fed.

As to the recipes given by Rumpolt, many are either fairly
simple or obviously foreign in origin. The latter are often strangely
disguised: a *holopotrida* is not a Greek quadruped, but the Spanish
olla podrida, a well-known dish which both Samuel Pepys and
John Evelyn ate in England. Its chief attraction for the cook was

Figure 9 A merchant's dinner, from Max Rumpolt's cookery book.

the number of possible combinations of ingredients: Rumpolt lists ninety items which could be included. There is also a hotchpotch (*Hudtspudt*) which is reminiscent of the one given in, of all places, a sermon by the Strassburg preacher Johann Geiler, printed under the delightful title *A Hare in Pepper* in 1502. *Hotzenblotz*, as Geiler calls it, is made by cutting up a cold chicken in a casserole, adding onions cut in rounds, and pouring over strong vinegar, stirring as necessary.

Another clerical source of recipes is a manuscript found in the buildings of the Dominican monastery of St Paul at Leipzig in the nineteenth century, which dates from the mid-sixteenth century. It contains a number of Polish and Hungarian recipes, as well as more homely fare, such as the chicken stew for which the recipe was 'given to me by my aunt Walpurgis Hartmann, a most excellent cook'. The anonymous writer adds other comments of this kind: *Galgenmuss* (gallows dish), a kind of sweet omelette, is so called because 'a poor sinner called Lehmann ate it as he went to the gallows'. Roast figs, in a recipe rather like the medieval English one on p. 96, were 'a special favourite with Bishop John, who had been told about them by a pious brother on his return from Palestine. In Asia the Arabs and infidels eat them on fast days – but that is no reason for a pious Christian soul to take fright at them.' Other dishes came from nearby monasteries, or were brought back by monks who had been on their travels, such as another chicken stew which is noted as a 'Slovenian dish'. The cook himself – or perhaps he was more a steward than a cook – had seen the world too: he talks of eating a burbot at the table of a country nobleman near Brandenburg, so large that its liver alone weighed over a pound. He ends rather sadly with a lament over the difficulties of running a kitchen, complaining that it is difficult to get the meat roasted properly, that proper equipment is lacking; but he obviously took pride in his work.

At the end of the century, we find a German merchant's wife buying a variety of exotic items. Frau Magdalena Paumgartner, writing to her husband on his travels in Italy and elsewhere, asks for such items as artichoke seeds, lemons, oranges, Italian melons, pistachios and olive oil, as well as cucumber and cauliflower seeds. The artichoke also appears in a bourgeois menu of the period, perhaps for a wedding or other special occasion:

First course: (Voressen) small fish in different sauces, beef with raisins, almonds and spices, two blackcock, calves' head and tripe

Second course: chicken soup, capons, veal with noodles, beef, smoked meat, hot boiled carp, trout, almond tart, marzipan, and artichokes if the season was right

Third course: cabbage, which consisted of shredded cabbage with bacon; round the edge of the dish were slices of bread roll spread with brains, with a piece of roast veal or leg of chamois

Fourth course: this was a drinking session, accompanied by egg cakes, a boiled crab or a game pie

The meal ended with cheese and fruit.

Renaissance Recipes

ITALIAN

CATALAN MIRAUSO

[for 4 persons]

This recipe and the following one are Spanish in origin.

2½ lb chicken	½ tsp cinnamon
2 slices lightly toasted brown bread	1 tbsp vinegar
1 dsp sugar	3 egg yolks
2 oz roast almonds	½ tsp ginger
¾ pt stock	

Roast the chicken for 30 minutes on the spit or in a moderate oven without covering. Put in a casserole. Meanwhile, roast the almonds under the grill until just brown (2–3 minutes), and toast the bread. Crumble the bread and mix with the almonds and egg yolks. Season. Add the vinegar and stock. Mix the cinnamon, ginger and sugar, and sprinkle into the mixture. Add to the casserole, and cook for one hour in the oven at Regulo Mark 3 (320°).

Giovane, *Opera Dignissima, c.* 1630

SALSO DE PAVON

1 egg yolk, hard-boiled	1 pinch saffron
1 tsp sugar	2 oz roast almonds
1½ tbs vinegar	⅛ tsp ginger
⅛ tsp cinnamon	2 tbs uncooked grape juice
1 chicken liver	

Pound hard-boiled yolk, liver and almonds with vinegar and grape juice. Add cinnamon, ginger and sugar. Colour with saffron, and put in a small saucepan to simmer for 3–5 minutes. Serve with roast chicken or other bland meats such as pork or veal.

Ibid

SUPPA MAGRA INGLESE [for 4 persons]

2 pts salted water	1 lb parsnips
2 oz butter	¼ tsp ginger
2 yolks of egg	¼ pt grape juice

Bring salted water to boil. Add parsnips, which should be scraped and the centre part removed, then chopped. Stir in ginger and butter. Simmer for 20 minutes. Beat yolks of egg, and add these and grape juice. Simmer for a further 2–3 minutes, and serve with pieces of bread in the dishes.

Messi Sbugo, *Conviti, c.* 1555

FRIED HAM [for 4 persons]

2 lb ham	¼ glass cooked grape juice
¼ tsp cinnamon	pepper
½ tsp sage	½ glass wine vinegar

Cut ham into not very thin slices, and put in frying pan without fat added. Cook until lightly brown, and then add remaining ingredients. Simmer for 15 minutes. Allow to cool, remove any excess fat from liquid, and serve cold.

Romoli, *Singolar Dottrina*

FRATI FRITTERS [for 2 persons]

3 eggs	2 oz butter
2 tsp rosemary	3 oz white breadcrumbs
1 tsp tarragon	¼ tsp pepper
1 tsp thyme	¼ tsp cinnamon
¼ pt sweet white wine	2 tsp grated parmesan

Fry herbs lightly in butter, without browning. If fresh herbs are used, increase quantities to about 1 tbs each. Allow to cool, beat lightly with the eggs, and add cinnamon, pepper, wire and breadcrumbs. Allow to stand for 1 hour. Add grated parmesan. Fry in fresh butter, making fritters about 1 inch thick.

Ibid

STUFFED EGGS [for 4 persons]

8 hard-boiled eggs	2 oz cream cheese
2 oz butter	2 crushed cloves
¼ tsp pepper	1 raw egg
1 tsp grated parmesan	½ tsp cinnamon

Halve eggs lengthwise, take out yolk. Mix with butter, cheese, pepper, cinnamon and cloves. Beat the raw egg and moisten mixture with this. Refill eggs with mixture, fry upside down in butter for 2–3 minutes. Add parmesan on top and grill until brown.

Ibid

MINUTAL [for 4 persons]

1 cabbage   *3 pts salted water*
2 tbs sugar

Slice cabbage one inch thick. Bring water to boil, put in cabbage and cook briefly for 1–2 minutes. Drain and chop finely, pound in mortar. Add sugar and boil for further 10 minutes.

Platina, *De Honesta Voluptate,* 1472

EGGS IN THE FLORENTINE MANNER

'Put one by one fresh eggs into a pan containing hot oil; keep each one as nearly circular as possible by keeping the white in shape with a spoon. The yolks should be soft inside. This is more difficult than it might seem.'

Ibid

PARSLEY BROTH [for 4 persons]

Called *brodo apostolorum* 'the apostles' soup'

$\frac{3}{4}$ *lb mutton*   *pinch saffron*
$\frac{1}{4}$ *pt grape juice*   *1 dsp vinegar*
$\frac{1}{4}$ *tsp pepper* $\frac{1}{2}$ *lb smoked sausage*
4 tbs chopped parsley $\frac{1}{8}$ *tsp cinnamon*
$\frac{1}{2}$ *lb pork*   *2 pts salted water*

Cut the meat into cubes and slice the sausage. Bring water to boil, and add meat and sausages, saffron, pepper and cinnamon, and grape juice and vinegar. Simmer for $1\frac{1}{2}$ hours. Add chopped parsley and other herbs to taste. Bring to boil and serve at once in dishes containing pieces of bread.

Scappi, *Opera,* 1570

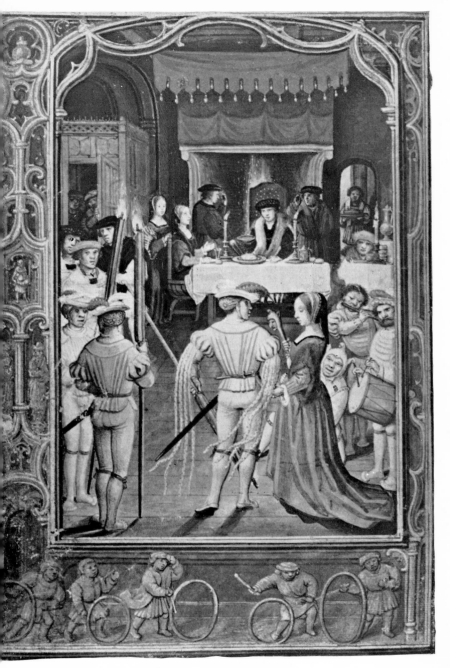

11. A feast by candle-light in the early sixteenth century.

FRENCH

BASIC STOCK

¾ lb beef, preferably on the bone; ¼ lb shallots
  otherwise use stewing steak and 1 dsp salt
  separate bone ¼ lb mutton
1 tbs chopped parsley ½ uncooked chicken
2 crushed cloves 1 tsp thyme
3 pts water

Bring salted water to boil and add all ingredients. Boil for 3¾–4 hours.
Strain through sieve and keep in refrigerator.

La Varenne, Le Vray Cuisinier, 1653

JOINT OF MUTTON À LA DAUBE [for 4–6 persons]

4 rashers fat bacon 3 lb leg of lamb
½ pt white wine bouquet garni
peel of 1 lemon 3 pts salted water

Simmer bacon for 10 minutes in unsalted water. Bring 3 pts salted water
to boil. Lard lamb with strips of bacon and season. Put in water and
simmer for 60–70 minutes. Add white wine, lemon peel and bouquet
garni. Simmer for a further 30 minutes, drain and serve, carving in
fairly thick slices.

Ibid

JOINT OF MUTTON 'AFTER THE LEGATE'S WAY'
[for 4–6 persons]

4 rashers fat bacon 3 lb leg of lamb
2 crushed cloves ½ lb mushrooms
1 tbs basic stock (see above) 1 lb artichoke hearts
1 lb sweetbreads ½ tsp tarragon
½ tsp rosemary bay leaf
lemon for garnish truffle if available
salt, pepper ½ tsp capers

Simmer bacon for 10 minutes in unsalted water. Lard lamb with strips
of bacon and season. Put in frying pan and brown lightly. Take out,
put in casserole. Add stock, salt, pepper, cloves, herbs, mushrooms
and capers. Seal lid with flour and water, and cook for 3 hours in oven
at Regulo Mark 3 (320°). Cook sweetbreads by simmering in salted
water for 10 minutes, and add these and artichoke hearts just before
serving. Garnish with lemon.

Ibid

LOIN OF PORK WITH A SAUCE ROBERT

La Varenne's original instructions are as follows:
'Lard it with great lard, then rost it, and baste it with verjuice and vineager, with a bundle of sage. After the fat is fallen, take it for to fry an onion with, which being fryed, you shall put under the loyn, with the sauce wherewith you have basted it. All being a little stoved together, serve.' [Contemporary English translation]

[for 4 persons]

2 lb loin of pork	*4 rashers fat bacon*
1 tbs vinegar	*2 tbs dry cider*
1 tsp sage	*1 onion*

Simmer bacon for 10 minutes in unsalted water. Lard pork, and preheat oven to Regulo Mark 2 (310°). Put pork in roasting tray with cider and vinegar and sage. Cook for 1¾ hours, basting four or five times. Take out of oven, skim off fat, reserve the rest of the stock. Fry onion in the fat, and put under the pork with the rest of the juices. Put back in oven for a further thirty minutes. Serve, using stock as gravy.

Ibid

LIVER OF VEAL STICKED [for 2 persons]

1 calf's liver	*pepper*
3 tbs vinegar	*1 crushed clove*
¼ tsp allspice	*1 small onion*
juice ½ orange	*salt*
¼ tsp sage	*juice ½ lemon*
2 rashers bacon, fat only	*½ tsp rosemary*

Put vinegar, pepper, salt, allspice, clove, juice of lemon and orange, sliced onion, rosemary and sage in a small bowl, stir well and leave to stand for two hours. Lard the liver with bacon fat by threading it through. Put under grill and cook on low setting, basting with vinegar mixture, until pale brown (about 10–15 minutes).

Ibid

POTAGE À LA REINE [for 4 persons]

2½ lb chicken	*1 pt basic stock (as p. 121)*
2 oz flaked almonds	*bouquet garni*
6 hard-boiled egg yolks	*mushroom stuck with cloves*
croutons	

Roast chicken for half normal roasting time, i.e. 25–30 minutes on spit or in oven at Regulo Mark 5 (360°). Carve, and pound flesh in mortar. Add almonds, egg yolks, mushroom and stock and bouquet garni, and put in casserole. Simmer for 30–40 minutes, and remove mushroom before serving and add croutons.

De Lune, *Le Nouveau Cuisinier*, 1660

BEEF À LA MODE

This is for use in a stew or pasty. A similar technique was probably used by Samuel Pepys's cousin Thomas when Pepys dined with him on 6 January 1660, though Pepys saw through the deception and noted that 'the venison pasty was palpable beef, which was not handsome'. The flavour is good, but only remotely similar to venison.

½ *lb rump steak, cut thick*	*salt*
juice 1 lemon	*1½ glasses dry cider*
bay leaf	*pepper*
3 tbs vinegar	*bacon*

Beat the steak flat, and marinate in the remaining ingredients for 2 hours. Lard with bacon and cook according to any stew recipe which requires long, slow cooking.

Cuisinier Methodique, 1662

STUFFED MUSHROOMS   [for 4 persons]

½ *lb large button mushrooms*	*4 oz butter*
¼ *tsp marjoram*	¼ *tsp thyme*
1 egg yolk	*salt*
2 oz pork fat	*1 shallot*
4 oz minced chicken	

Mix minced chicken, fat, salt, herbs and chopped shallot and bind with an egg yolk. Stuff peeled and washed mushrooms, arranging them in a flat earthenware dish and placing the mixture on top with a teaspoon. Melt butter and pour into dish. Cover and cook in oven at Regulo Mark 2 (310°) for 40 minutes. These can be served hot or cold.

Ibid

POTAGE À LA FANTASQUE   [for 2 persons]

¼ *lb stewing steak*	¼ *pt milk*
¼ *tsp pepper*	¼ *tsp cinnamon*
salt	¼ *tsp ginger*
¼ *pt wine*	*1 tsp sugar*

Cut meat into 1-inch cubes. Put with remaining ingredients into saucepan and bring to boil. Simmer gently for 35–40 minutes, stirring occasionally.

Ibid

CREAM OF MELON [for 4 persons]

1 melon (not over-ripe)   *3 oz sugar*
¼ pt white wine   *grated lemon peel*
½ tsp cinnamon

Halve melon, take out seeds, and cut out flesh. Put in a medium saucepan with the other ingredients, and cook slowly until the sugar is dissolved, stirring continuously. Put through a fine sieve, reheat and cook slowly, continuing to stir until thick.

De Lune, *Le Nouveau Cuisinier*, 1660

NULLE [for 2 persons]

4 egg yolks   *pinch of salt*
1 egg white   *4 oz caster sugar*
½ pt cream

Beat the cream, egg yolks, egg white, salt and sugar together, and strain the mixture through a sieve. Preheat oven to Regulo Mark 2 (310°) and fill a 2-inch-deep baking pan with boiling water. Place this in the oven. Pour the mixture into a suitable fireproof dish so that it is about 2½ inches deep. Place this in the baking pan, and cook for about 1 hour until firm.

La Varenne, *Le Vray Cuisinier*

SAVOY BISCUIT [for 4 persons]

4 eggs   *½ tsp aniseed*
6 oz flour   *½ lb sugar*

Mix the aniseed and flour, separate one of the eggs and keep the yolk for glazing. Sift into a bowl, make a small well in the centre and break the remaining eggs into this adding the extra egg white; draw the flour in slowly and then add the sugar. Put mixture on a greased baking tray in teaspoonfuls, to make a flat biscuit about 3-inch diameter. Bake in oven at Regulo Mark 2 (310°) for 30 minutes. Take out, glaze lightly by brushing on egg yolk, and return to oven for a further 15 minutes.

Ibid

GERMAN

GREAT EGGS

Break tip neatly off eggs, put in a little thyme, salt and cinnamon. Stir with a skewer until thoroughly mixed. Seal top with egg white, and bake in a moderate oven (Regulo Mark 5, 360°) for 20 minutes.

Koch und Kellermeisterei, 1554

AN EXCELLENT DISH WITH PASTRY [for 2 persons]

2 hard-boiled eggs   ½ lb pastry
¼ pt milk   saffron
4 baked apples

Hardboil eggs and bake apples. Separate egg yolks and whites. Add pinch of saffron to milk, and bring to boil. Boil until slightly reduced, and mix with egg yolks. Peel, core and chop apples and add to yolks and milk. Make rounds of pastry, and fill these like sandwiches with the mixture. Place on a greased baking tray and bake for 20 minutes at Regulo Mark 5 (360°). Chop the egg whites and scatter on top before serving.

Ibid

BAKED RICE [for 4 persons]

This makes an excellent base for stews or soups, as an alternative to the usual trencher or sop (a piece of bread) which would have been used. It is rather like the Italian *polenta* in consistency.

4 oz rice flour   2 eggs

Beat rice flour and eggs together, and fry in butter as flat cakes until lightly browned.

Ibid

A BLACK MUESLI [for 4–6 persons]

½ lb black grapes   1 oz sugar
2 apples   ½ lb oatmeal
2 pears   ½ pt water

Boil pears and apples until soft. Peel, core and chop into cubes. Pip and halve grapes. Mix fruit, sugar and oatmeal, and add water. Bring to the boil, stirring continuously. Serve with milk and sugar to taste.

Ibid

English Cookery in the Sixteenth and Seventeenth Centuries

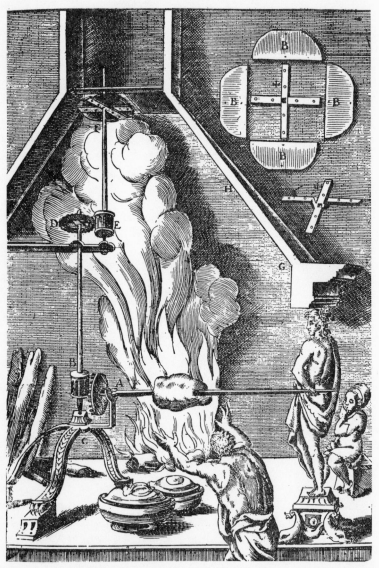

Figure 10 A smokejack, or turnspit worked by smoke, 1656. A very large fire was needed to make the device effective.

Nowadays, if the table be not covered from the one end to the other, as thick as one dish can stand by another, with delicate meats of sundry sorts, one clean different from another, and to every dish a several sauce appropriate to his kinde, it is thought there unworthy the name of a dinner. Yea, so many dishes shall you have pestering the table at once, as the insatiablest *Helluo*, the devouringest glutton, or the greediest cormorant that is, can scarce eat of every one a little. And these many shall you have at the first course, as many at the second; and, peradventure, more at the third; besides other sweet condiments, and delicate confections of spiceries, and I cannot tell what. And to these dainities, all kind of wines are not wanting, you may be sure. Oh, what nicety is this! what vanity, excess, riot and superfluity is here! Oh, farewell former world! For I have heard my father say that in his dayes, one dish or two of good wholesome meat was thought sufficient for a man of great worship to dine withal; and if they had three or four kinds, it was reputed a sumptuous feast. A good piece of beef was thought then good meat, and able for the best; but now it is thought too gross, for their tender stomachs are not able to digest such crude and harsh meats.

Philip Stubbes's complaint against the extravagances of Elizabethan nobles would have found a better target, one feels, in the far more lavish displays of the Italians whom they imitated. For English cooking, after its first triumphant flourish in the early fifteenth century, became incurably domestic; it rose only to state occasions by borrowing from the French. The cookery books are all on a humble scale, often as small as twenty-four pages; there is nothing to compare with Scappi, Frugoli or Rumpolt until after the Restoration. The earliest printed cookery book in England is *A Proper Newe Booke of Cookerye* of 1545, the first of a series of booklets or short compilations with similar titles, and often containing the same recipes, which were part of the Elizabethan printer-publisher's stock-in-trade. Most of the dishes are simplified versions of medieval dishes, with fewer spices, but the same tendency to present everything as a hash or a gruel. The roast beef which Stubbes laments does not appear in the books; but then it was not a 'made dish' and no housewife would have turned to a book to find instructions on how to prepare it.

Something of foreign ways nonetheless infiltrated into English kitchens. The tales of Henry VIII's love of food are a mixture of Gargantuan appetite and Sybarite luxury; he is said to have rewarded the inventor of a new pudding by giving him a manor. But his display and pageantry, though on a magnificent scale in terms of clothes, jewelry and architectural fantasies for occasions such as the Field of the Cloth of Gold, left no mark on the way in which his cooks and their successors prepared the royal food. Elizabeth I's dining habits, too, were calculated more as a ceremony than as a gastronomic event. The German traveller, Paul Hentzner, left a vivid description of her at table:

A gentleman entered the room bearing a rod, and along with him another who had a table-cloth, which after they had both kneeled three times with the utmost veneration, he spread upon the table, and after kneeling again, they both retired. Then came two others, one with the rod again, the other with a salt-cellar, a plate and bread; when they had kneeled, as the others had done, and placed what was brought upon the table, they too retired with the same ceremonies performed by the first. At last came an unmarried lady (we were told she was a countess) and along with her a married one, bearing a tasting-knife; the former was dressed in white silk, who, when she had prostrated herself three times in the most graceful manner, approached the table, and rubbed the plates with bread and salt, with as much awe as if the queen had been present: when they had waited at there a little while, the yeomen of the guards entered, bareheaded, clothed in scarlet, with a golden rose upon their backs, bringing in at each turn a course of twenty-four dishes, served in plate, most of it gilt; these dishes were received by a gentleman in the same order they were brought, and placed upon the table, while the lady-taster gave to each of the guard a mouthful to eat, of the particular dish he had brought for fear of any poison. During the time that this guard . . . were bringing dinner, twelve trumpets and two kettle-drums made the hall ring for half an hour together. At the end of all the ceremonial a number of unmarried ladies appeared, and with particular solemnity, lifted the meat off the table, and conveyed it into the queen's inner and more private chamber, where, after she had chosen for herself, the rest goes to the ladies of the court. The queen dines and sups alone, with very few attendants; and it is very seldom that any body, foreigner or native, is admitted at that time.

It was Elizabeth's nobles who found out the new continental fashions and tried to transplant them. Surrey's poetry in the Italian manner and Lyly's stylized comedies were important in their day, but their innovations in the kitchen did not meet with much

13. *Above* A seventeenth-century French kitchen scene, showing elaborate *patisserie* in preparation.

14. *Right* Title page of La Varenne's *Le Pastissier François*. The making of pasties belonged to the pastry-cook's work; hence the game-birds on the wall for the meat fillings.

LE
PASTISSIER
FRANÇOIS.

A Amsterdam,
Chez Louys et Daniel Elzevier. A. 1655.

15. A French feast in the late seventeenth century; note the enormous amount of food on the tables.

success. William Harrison describes the nobles' diet in terms similar to Stubbes's:

In number of dishes and change of meat, the nobilitie of England, (whose cookes are for the most part musicall-headed Frenchmen and strangers) doo most exceed, sith there is no daie in maner that passeth over their heads, wherein they have not onelie beefe, mutton, veale, lambe kind, porke, conie, capon, pig, or so manie of these as the season yeeldeth; but also some portion of the red or fallow deere, beside great varietie of fish and wild foule, and thereto sundrie other delicates wherein the sweet hand of the seafaring Portingale [Portuguese] is not wanting: so that for a man to dine with one of them and to taste of everie dish that standeth before him (which few use to doo, but ech one feedeth upon that meat him best liketh for the time) . . . is rather to yeeld unto a conspiracie with a great deale of meat for the speedie suppression of naturall health.

Harrison does go on to say that the nobleman and their guests do not eat as much as might be expected, and the reason for all this plenty is the number of unexpected visitors every day, as well as provision for the servants and the poor who get the leftovers. But neither he nor Stubbes complains of any over-refinement of taste, and even the quantities consumed, when we look at actual accounts, seem to have been quite modest. The household book of the fifth Earl of Northumberland in 1512 shows a typical breakfast as a simple enough meal: half a chine of mutton, a sliced loaf, two white rolls, a quart of beer and a quart of wine are to be provided for the earl and countess, except in Lent when salt fish, 'baconned herring' (i.e. kippers) and sprats replace the meat. Even this meal is served only four days a week; on Mondays, Wednesdays and Fridays the provisions were even less. An eighteenth-century farmer would have regarded this as a modest start to the day. In the middle of the sixteenth century, Sir William Petre's household accounts from Ingatestone show a fairly wide range of foodstuffs, but nothing particularly spectacular. The main meat was mutton, followed by beef, venison and pork in about equal quantities. Eggs and cheese were much used, particularly the latter: the proportion is about one pound of cheese to every egg. Pigeon figures largely, for in one year over a thousand were taken from the dovecot during the summer months; and the steward had a regular contract for the supply of wildfowl at agreed prices. Fish came from the east coast – oysters, flatfish and mackerel, but the carp pond was the chief source of supply, and there was also the occasional bass or salmon. Petre seems to have observed fish-days fairly regularly, in obedience to the recent acts which declared them necessary for the fishing industry; but anyone who held them to be necessary on religious grounds was open to prosecution for heresy. Another set of accounts, those of 'Wild' Darrell for a visit to London in 1589, show that he ate fish six times on twelve Fridays.

As far as we can tell from Petre's spice account, the cooking of the food was still much in the medieval manner. On 1 April 1549 'provision of spice' included: ½ lb mace, ½ lb cloves, 1 oz saffron, 20 lb currants, 4 lb dates, 1 lb ginger, ½ lb cinnamon, 6 lb pepper, 1 lb box biscuits, 1 lb carraway, 6 lb almonds, ¾ hundreth great raisins, 3 lb rice.

Early in Elizabeth's reign, Sir William Petre was visited by the queen; but he got off lightly, for her progresses had not yet become the lavish occasions of the 1590s, culminating in such episodes as Sir Henry Lee's great entertainment at Ditchley in 1591, a combination of festival, tournament, masque and banquet in honour of 'Gloriana'. As John Nichols says in his history of Elizabeth's journeyings through the kingdom, apropos of the later occasions:

Where the Queen paraded through a country town, almost every Pageant was a Pantheon; even the pastrycooks were expert mythologists: at dinner select transformations of Ovid's Metamorphoses were exhibited in confectionery and the splendid iceing of an immense historic plumb-cake was embossed with a delicious basso-rilievo of the destruction of Troy.

Perhaps it was these conceits that were the concern of the 'musicall-headed French cooks', since they have left so little trace elsewhere. Ben Jonson aptly sums up the qualities required to mount such displays of the cook's art:

> A master cook! why, he is the man of men,
> He's a professor; he designs, he draws,
> He paints, he carves, he builds, he fortifies,
> Makes citadels of curious fowl and fish.

Some he dry-ditches, some motes round with broths,
Mounts marrow-bones, cuts fifty-angled custards,
Rears bulwark pies; and for his outer works,
He raiseth ramparts of immortal crust,
And teacheth all the tactics at one dinner—
What ranks, what files, to put his dishes in,
The whole art military! Then he knows
The influence of the stars upon his meats,
And all their seasons, tempers, qualities;
And so to fit his relishes and sauces.
He has nature in a pot 'bove all the chemists
The bare-breech'd brethren of the rosy cross.
He is an architect, an engineer,
A soldier, a physician, a philosopher,
A general mathematician.

Rober May, writing in 1660, looked back to these feasts with nostalgia, though the pie which he describes would certainly not have pleased Elizabeth:

Triumphs and trophies in Cookery, to be used at Festival Times, as Twelfth-day, &c.

Make the likeness of a Ship in Paste-board, with Flags and Streamers, the Guns belonging to it of Kickses [kickshaws], bind them about with packthread, and cover them with close paste proportionable to the fashion of a Cannon with Carriages, lay them in places convenient as you see them in Ships of war, with such holes and trains of powder that they may all take fire; Place your Ship firm in the great Charger; then make a salt round about it, and stick therein egg-shells full of sweet water, you may by a great Pin take all the meat out of the egg by blowing, and then fill it up with the rose-water, then in another Charger have the proportion of a Stag made of coarse paste, with a broad Arrow in the side of him, and his body filled up with claret-wine; in another Charger at the end have the proportion of a Castle with Battlements, Portcullices, Gates and Draw-Bridges made of Paste-board, the Guns and Kickses, and covered with coarse paste as the former; place it at a distance from the ship to fire at each other. The Stag being placed betwixt them with egg shells full of sweet water placed in salt. At each side of the Charger wherein is the Stag, place a Pye made of coarse paste filled with bran, and yellowed over with saffron or the yolks of eggs, gild them over in spots, as also the Stag, the Ship, and Castle; bake them, and place them with gilt bay-leaves on turrets and tunnels of the Castle and Pyes; being baked, make a hole in the bottom of your pyes, take out the bran, put in your Frogs, and Birds, and close up the holes with the same coarse paste, then cut the Lids neatly up; To be taken off the Tunnels; being all placed in order upon the Table, before you fire the trains of powder, order it so that some of the Ladies may be persuaded to pluck the Arrow out of the Stag, then will the Claret-wine follow, as blood that runneth out of a wound. This being done with admiration to the beholders, after some short pause, fire the train of the Castle, that the pieces all of one side may go off, then fire the Trains of one side of the Ship as in a battle; next turn the chargers; and by degrees fire the trains of each other side as before. This done, to sweeten the stink of powder, let the Ladies take the egg-shells full of sweet-waters and throw them at each other. All dangers being seemingly over, by this time you may suppose they will desire to see what is in the pyes; where lifting first the lid off one pye, out skip some Frogs; which make the Ladies to skip and shriek; next after the other pye, whence come out the birds,* who by a natural instinct flying in the light, will put out the Candles, so that what with the flying Birds and skipping Frogs, the one above, the other beneath, will cause much delight and pleasure to the whole company: at length the Candles are lighted, and a banquet brought in, the Musick sounds, and every one with much delight and content rehearses their actions in the former passages. These were formerly the delights of the Nobility, before good House-keeping had left *England*, and the Sword really acted that which was only counterfeited in such honest and laudable exercises as these.

But there were soberer minds at work on the subject of food, doctors and physicians who studied diet as an aspect of medicine. One of them, Andrew Boorde, produced *A Dietary of Helthe* in 1542, which 'treateth of wylde fowle, tame fowle, Byrdes of frutes, (and fyrst of fygges) of herbes and of a general dyet, for all manner of men and women, being sycke or hole'. Although the book itself is respectable enough, its author had a chequered career: intermittently a Carthusian monk, he was also a royal 'agent' abroad, a doctor at Glasgow University, went on pilgrimage to Jerusalem and was finally imprisoned in his fifties on a charge of scandalous living. His book was the first of a number in a similar

---

* This was an old joke. The earliest mention I can find of it is in a fourteenth-century romance, where as soon as the pies were opened, falcons, merlins and other hawks set off in pursuit of the birds. Compare also Trimalchio's pig stuffed with thrushes—though this is probably Petronius's own invention.

vein, which remained popular throughout the sixteenth and seventeenth centuries. Henry Buttes, a fellow of Corpus Christi College, Cambridge, provided one of the liveliest and most informative in the genre, spiced with a donnish wit. He entitled it: *Dyets dry dinner: consisting of eight severall courses all served after the order of time universall.* His preface tells us much about local dishes and preferences:

Welcome courteous countrymen. I meane especially *Norfolkmen,* for they are true Catholiques in matter of Dyet: no Recusants fo any thing that is mans meate. I bid all in general, excepting only such as are affrayed of roasted Pigge, or breast or legge of Mutton, a Ducke &c. To conclude, I forbid no man, but him onely that hath maried a wife & cannot come. No man shall loose his labour. Here are *Lettuses* for every mans lips. For the *Northern-man, white-meates, Beefe, Mutton, Venison:* for the *Southerne-man, Fruites, Hearbes, Fowle, Fish, Spice* and *Sauce.* As for the *Middle-sex* or *Londoner.* I smell his Diet. *Vescitur auraætheria.** Here is a Pipe of right *Trinidado*** for him. The *Yorkers* they will bee contente with bald *Tabacodocks.*† What should I say? Here is good *Veale* for the *Essex man*: passing *Leekes* and excellent *Cheese* for the *Welsh-man. Denique quod non?* Mary, here are neither *Eg-pies* for the *Lancashire-man,* nor *Wag-tayles* for the *Kentish-man* . . .

He then analyses the 'choice, use, hurt and correction' of foods, all in the same vein: 'All say a Lemon in wine is good; some thinke a Leman [i.e. mistress] and wine better.' He recommends various ways of preparing food, though none amounts to a recipe: quinces are to be boiled well with honey, walnuts eaten with a little garlic. He also retains some of the old ideas about suitable foods for different classes, as for example with pheasant:

Choise Fat, gotten in hawking in winter.
Use Good in hecticke fevers: restoreth their strength that are in recovery: of singular goood nourishment: helpeth a weake stomache.
Hurt It only makes the Swaine, short winded.
Correction Therefore good Peasant
    Touch not the Pheasant
    But save thy weasant [gullet]
    Y'are somewhat pleasant [foolish]

* 'Let him live on heaven's air' (cf. Vergil, Aeneid, 1, 546
** Cured tobacco
† Tobacco leaves

Buttes's book belonged in the study rather than the kitchen. Practical books appear in quantity from 1575 onwards. Even though these are mostly written by men, they are aimed at the mistress of the house: *A Good Hous-wives Treasury, The Good Huswives Handmaid, for Cookerie in her Kitchen, The Good Huswife's Jewell,* and even *The Widdowes Treasure,* which contains among the remedies which make up most of the book one marvellous physic, sovereign remedy against not only Elizabethan cookery but absentmindedness as well:

This decoction is good to eate both before and after meate
For it will make digestion good, and turne your meate to pure blood
Besides all this it doth excell, all windines to expell.
And all groce humours colde and rawe, that are in belly, stomacke or
    mawe.
It will dissolve without paine and keep ill vapors from the braine.
Besides all this it will restore your memory though lost before.

All of which is wrought by a concoction of pepper, aniseed, ginger and sugar.

These compilations were revised and reissued at frequent intervals: *A Book of Cookerie* went through a number of editions between 1590 and 1620 before it became *A New Booke of Cookerie,* alias *The Good Huswives Handmaid.* This work limits itself to the kitchen; and the new recipes are attributed to their sources, rather as *The Parisian Housekeeper* had acknowledged Hotin's recipes two hundred years earlier. Thus we have 'To boil a capon with oranges after Mistress Duffield's way', or 'The keeping of lard after my Lady Marquesse of Dorset's way'. Quantities begin to be given, and there is an air of practical instruction absent from older sources. The cook is assumed to have some basic knowledge but not to be master of a great deal of lore about spices or the cooking of different kinds of dish. Many dishes were served on sops (pieces of bread)* and continued to be presented like this until the Victorian era and the widespread use of potato. Thickenings consisted of breadcrumbs and egg yolks, as in medieval kitchens, though the more expensive rice flour beloved of the medieval court cook does not reappear in these humbler circles.

One aspect of the cook's art which recurs throughout these

---

* A sop was placed in the dish; a trencher served as the dish itself.

books is the problem of preserving and candying, which cooks in the great households would have been accustomed to doing as a matter of course. The ordinary housewife, with smaller quantities to deal with, would need instruction in the secrets of the still-room, as some items would only occasionally come her way, and her experience of the more unusual confections would be limited. So her needs were supplied by the authors of special works on preserving. Sir Hugh Plat's *Delights for Ladies,* one of the classics of its kind, places 'The art of preserving, conserving, candying &c.' and 'Secrets in distillation' before 'Cookeries and huswiferie'. He ends with a section of 'Sweete powders, oyntements, beauties &c.' dealing with the making of perfumes and cosmetics. Though such subjects had been written about abroad, notably by Michael Nostradamus, brother of the astrologer, at Lyon in the 1550s, this was the first English collection of such 'beauty aids' and as such was most successful. Plat also gives some recipes for cookery and mentions Scappi's book of 1570 on two occasions, one of the few direct acknowledgements to an Italian source.

Jacobean cookery shows little change from the Elizabethan manner, and works such as Murrell's *Two Books of Cookerie* merely hint at the 'now new English and French fashion', though the practice of boiling fish and poultry whole in a stock, and serving them in a sauce without cutting them up shows that the new style of eating with a fork had reached England in earnest. After the Restoration, however, there is a revolution in the English kitchen, brought about by the courtiers newly returned from exile with the taste of the latest French dishes still fresh in their memory. This current of fashion mingles with a number of other traits of the times in the work of Sir Kenelm Digby. Digby was a remarkable character, quite apart from his scientific and culinary work. Son of one of the men executed for their part in the Gunpowder Plot, he was given a cosmopolitan education, travelling to Madrid when he was fourteen and later going on an early version of the Grand Tour. He also studied under a doctor, Richard Napier, who lived near his home, and who gave him an abiding interest in alchemy and astrology. He married the famous beauty Venetia Stanley, despite the fact that she had been the Earl of Dorset's mistress. His adventures abroad included privateering and an embassy to the papal court in the course of which he took to arguing with and publicly contradicting the pope. After his wife's death he took up science in earnest and was one of the founders of the Royal Society. Though he seems to have been something of a showman, with a fondness for extraordinary tales – Evelyn called him 'an errant mountebank' – his learning was wide and the book published from his papers after his death in 1665, *The Closet of Sir Kenelm Digby Knight Opened*, contains a variety of recipes for food and drink and 'curious observations', a rather less well organized version of Sir Hugh Plat's work covering a much greater field. It includes the famous advice on how to make tea:

The Jesuits that came from China, Ann. 1664, told Mr Waller . . . in these parts . . . we let the hot water remain too long soaking upon the Tea, which makes it extract into itself the earthy parts of the herb. The water is to remain upon it no longer than whiles you can say the *Miserere* psalm very leisurely.

His cookery is drawn from French sources as well as native English recipes, but is on the whole rather disappointing for such a well-travelled and flamboyant character. There is more of the herbalist than the practical cook in his writing, and he is really interested in items such as this, an early chicken broth for invalids:

The Queen's ordinary *Bouillon de Santé* in a morning was thus. A Hen, a handful of Parsley, a sprig of Thyme, three of Spear-minth, a little balm, half a great Onion, a little Pepper & Salt & a Clove, as much water as would cover the Hen; & *this boiled to less than a pint, for one good Porrenger full*.

The section on drinks includes a vast number of recipes for metheglin, a drink similar to mead but made with a large quantity of herbs; one can only assume that Digby was especially partial to it. One amusing entry is an early appearance of whipped cream ('My Lord of St Albans cresme fouettée') to be beaten 'with a bundle of white hard rushes of such as they make whisks to brush cloaks'. Cream generally figures in far more recipes than before; and Samuel Pepys often had just a dish of cream for breakfast at about this time when he was in the country.

Two other members of the Royal Society made contributions to the art of cookery in its early days, when 'the improving of natural knowledge by experiments' could embrace everything from Newton on the laws of gravity to 'a very particular account of the making of the several sorts of bread in France, which is accounted the best place for bread in the world' which Samuel Pepys heard on 1 March 1665. The lecturer was John Evelyn the diarist; some thirty years later he produced another gastronomic work, *Acetaria, A Discourse of Sallets* (Salads). Though salads were referred to in Roman books, and continued to appear in the Middle Ages, it was the seventeenth century which really elaborated on the idea. Salvatore Massonio had produced a treatise on them in Venice in 1627, entitled *Archidipno,* or, the salad and its uses, and recipes for enormous compilations of every kind of cold meat and vegetable, such as this example from Robert May, were already appearing in the cookery books:

Take all manner of knots of buds of sallet herbs, buds of pot-herbs, or any green herbs, as sage, mint, balm, burnet, violet-leaves, red cole-worts streaked of divers fine colours, lettice, any flowers, blanched almonds, blue figs, raisins of the sun, currans, capers, olives; then dish the sallet in a heap or pile, being mixed with some of the fruits, and all finely washed and swung in a napkin, then about the centre lay first sliced figs, next capers, and currans then almonds and raisins, next olives, and lastly either jagged beats, jagged lemons, hagged cucumbers, or cabbidge lettice in quarters, good oyl and wine vinegar, sugar or none.

Evelyn lists seventy-three herbs and plants as possible ingredients, which he puts into a table of combinations; he also gives other pieces of salad-making advice. Of garlic, he says:

We absolutely forbid it entrance into our *Salleting,* by reasons of its intolerable rankness, and which made it so detested of old, that the eating of it was (as we read) part of the punishment for such as had committed the horrid'st crimes. To be sure, tis not for Ladies Palats, nor those who court them, further than to permit a light touch on the Dish, with a *Clove* thereof.

He advises a porcelain or delft bowl, into which he measures his ingredients by 'pugils' (a pinch, plucked between thumb and fore-finger) and 'fascicules' or fistfuls.

The experiments carried out by Denys Papin and demonstrated to the Royal Society were more directly scientific in the modern

Species — Ordering and Culture.

No.	Species	Ordering and Culture.
1.	Endive,	}
2.	Cichory,	} Tied-up to Blanch.
3.	Sellery;	}
4.	Sweet-Fennel,	Earth'd-up.
5.	Rampions,	
6.	Roman } Lettuce,	}
7.	Cosse }	} Tied-up to Blanch.
8.	Silesian }	
9.	Cabbage }	
10.	Lob-Lettuce,	Tied close up.
11.	Corn-Sallet,	Pome and Blanch of themselves.
12.	Purslane,	Leaves, all of a midling size.
13.	Cresses broad,	Seed-Leaves, and the next to them.
14.	Spinach, curled,	The fine young Leaves only, with the first Shoots.
15.	Sorrel, French,	
16.	Sorrel, Greenland,	Only the tender young Leaves.
17.	Radish,	The Seed-Leaves, and those only next them.
18.	Cresses,	
19.	Turnep,	The Seed-Leaves only.
20.	Mustard,	
21.	Scurvy-grass,	
22.	Chervil,	The young Leaves immediately after the Seedlings.
23.	Burnet,	
24.	Rocket, Spanish,	
25.	Persly,	
26.	Tarragon,	The tender Shoots and Tops.
27.	Mints,	
28.	Sampier,	The young tender Leaves and Shoots.
29.	Balm,	
30.	Sage, Red,	
31.	Shalots,	The tender young Leaves.
32.	Cive and Onion,	
33.	Nasturtium; Indian	The Flowers and Bud-Flowers.
34.	Rampion, Belgrade,	The Seed-Leaves and young Tops.
35.	Trip-Madame,	

IX. Blanch'd.
XXVII. Green Unblanch'd.

January – May

Month.	Order. and Cult.	Species.	Proportion.
January,	Blanch'd as before	Rampions, Endive, Succory, Fennel, sweet, Sellery,	10, 2, 5, 1, 4 } Roots in Number.
		Lamb-Lettuce, Lob-Lettuce, Radish, Cresses,	A pugil of each.
February,		Turneps, Mustard Seedlings, Scurvy-grass, Spinach,	Three parts each.
	Green and Unblanch'd	Sorrel, Greenland, Sorrel, French, Chervil, sweet,	Of each One part.
		Burnet, Rocket,	Two parts.
		Tarragon, Mint, Balm, Sampier, Shalots, Cives,	One part of each.
and			Twenty large Leaves.
			One small part of each.
March.		Cabbage-Winter.	Very few.
			Two pugils or small handfuls.
April,	Blanch'd	Lop } Silesian Winter } Lettuce. Roman Winter	Of each a pugil.
		Radishes,	Three parts.
	Green Herbs Unblanch'd	Cresses, Purslan, Sorrel, French, Sampier,	Two parts. 1 Fasciat, or pretty full gripe. Two parts. One part.
May,			

June – December

Month.	Order and Cult.	Species.	Proportion.
and	Note, That the young Seedling Leaves of O-range and Lemon may all these Months be mingled with the Sallet.	Onions, young, Sage-tops, the Red, Parsley,	Six parts. Two parts.
		Cresses, the Indian, Lettuce, Belgrade, Trip-Madame, Chervil, sweet,	Of each One part.
June,		Burnet,	Two parts.
July,	Blanch'd, and may be eaten by themselves with some Nasturtium-Flowers.	Silesian Lettuce, Roman Lettuce, Cress,	One whole Lettuce. Two parts.
		Cabbage,	Four parts.
		Cresses, Nasturtium, Purslane,	Two parts. One part.
August,	Green Herbs by themselves, or mingl'd with the Blanch'd.	Lop-Lettuce, Belgrade, or Crumpen-Lettuce, Tarragon,	Two parts.
and		Sorrel, French, Burnet,	One part.
September.		Trip-Madame,	Two parts of each.
October,	Blanch'd	Endive, Sellery,	One part.
November,		Lop-Lettuce, Lambs-Lettuce, Radish, Cresses,	Two if large, four if small, Stalk and part of the Root and tenderest Leaves. An handful of each. Three parts. Two parts.
and	Green	Turnips, Mustard Seedlings,	One part of each.
December.		Cresses, broad, Spinach,	Two parts of each.

Figure 11 John Evelyn's table of instructions for making salads.

sense. Papin was a French physicist who worked with Sir Robert Boyle on the study of the vacuum, and in the course of his researches invented 'a New Digester', which was an early form of pressure cooker. He was much interested in the possibility of extracting nutrition from bones by softening them, and in the preservation of food, but improved and more rapid cooking was also one of his aims. The apparatus, though effective, was too complicated for everyday use, and its principles were not adopted in the kitchen until the arrival of the twentieth-century pressure-cooker. Other mechanical devices included clockwork and smoke-turned spits. The clockwork was used to raise a heavy weight which gradually descended again, turning gears as it went, while the smokejack relied on the draught up the chimney to turn a fan which then drove the spit, though it is doubtful how effective this was (see Fig. 10, p. 126).

Treatises like those of Evelyn and Papin were in the tradition of the learned amateur of the Renaissance, the gentleman who pursued knowledge for his own amusement. Among their forerunners had been such curiosities as Estienne d'Aigue's monograph on turtles and artichokes in 1549; contemporary works included Barra's work on the use of ice and its ill-effects, and Domenico Colmenero's treatise on the latest novelty from America, chocolate. Just as Evelyn had described an early coffee-drinker at Oxford, so Pepys recorded the arrival of tea and chocolate. Tea had first appeared in the late 1650s: 'that excellent and by all Physicians approved, China drink, called by the Chineans Tcha', as a newspaper advertisement described it. Chocolate had appeared a few years earlier, and Colmenero's treatise was translated into English for the benefit of the curious.

But it was professional cooks who made the greatest contribution in the English kitchen during the later seventeenth century. From the 1650s onwards, the chefs of leading noblemen began to record their secrets and to offer instruction in their mysteries much as the Italian cooks of the sixteenth century had done. The English writers, however, were much less inclined to stand on ceremony; there are no lengthy discussions of protocol, or advice to stewards on ordering banquets. These are books for use rather than study, much as the French cookery books – which they avowedly imitate – put food first and leave its presentation and serving to others.

At least two books which appeared at this time were direct translations from the French, the first examples of cookery crossing the frontiers since Platina had been put into French and German in the early fifteenth century. These were Monsieur Marnette's *The Perfect Cook* and Giles Rose's *Perfect School of Instruction for Officers of the Mouth*. The first part of Marnette's book is a translation of La Varenne's *Le Pastissier François,* and the *Perfect English Cook* which follows is very much in the French style. Giles Rose underlines some of the difficulties of translation when he gives a recipe for *carbonnade* which includes white powder, or *poudre blanche*. This ingredient baffled him, for he adds: 'What this White Powder is you must inform your self else-where; for I have enquired of a *French* Master Cook who told me plainly he could not inform me.' It seems likely that this is none other than the old medieval white powder or ground sugar, whose use was now relatively infrequent. Rose also includes the description of a French noble household from his original, which cannot have aroused much interest in the more informal circles of Charles II's court, where, as Pepys records, the lack of solemnity from the king downwards was frequently remarked upon.

Joseph Cooper's *The Art of Cooking Refined and Augmented* of 1654 is a fairly unremarkable book from someone who was 'chiefe cook to the late King'. Either Charles I liked plainer fare than his taste in other matters might lead us to expect, or the writer was anxious to prove that he was as good a Commonwealth citizen as the next man. Cooper's most interesting technique is a use of 'garnishes' fried in batter, which can be coloured green by adding spinach. A variety of main ingredients can be treated in this way, from oysters to sheeps' tongues, though whether these were then served as a kind of appetizer or as a side dish is not clear. The word originally meant a set of tableware – William Harrison talks of a garnish of pewter as containing twelve platters, twelve dishes and twelve saucers – but it was beginning to be used to mean 'ornament'; Cooper seems to have been the first to apply it to food.

A true professional cook's career is illustrated by the life of Robert May, whose *The Accomplisht Cook*, which we have already quoted, appeared in 1671. His father was a cook in the household of Lady Dormer, while he himself was sent as an apprentice to Paris, where he learnt his trade in the kitchen of the president of the Parlement. His work is the fruit of long service under many masters: he was in twelve different establishments, beginning with that of Lady Dormer, between his return to England in 1603 and his retirement in 1665, and he was eighty-four when the book appeared. It is one of the best works of the period, clear, comprehensive and not without humour and a little nostalgia for the days of Charles I. Nor is he a mere collector of recipes; these are the tried and tested procedures of a lifetime.

For elaborate collections of recipes were now good business for publishers. There are a number of compilations which seem to owe their existence to commercial motives rather than any real knowledge of the art. They are usually betrayed by their elaborate or pretentious titles; some are perfectly successful, as in the case of *The Queen's Closet Opened*, purporting to be the recipes and household lore of Charles I's consort, Henrietta Maria, which ran through a number of editions from its first appearance under the Commonwealth in 1654 – if kings were undesirable, royalist cookery at least seems to have been welcome. Equally royalist is the early Restoration book *The Court and Kitchen of Elizabeth, commonly called Joan Cromwell, the wife of the late usurper,* which puts a work on cookery to a new, and, so far as I know, unique use: political satire. The anonymous author declares roundly: 'Herein we do but retaliate . . . and repay in some sort, those many Libels, blasphemous Pamphlets & Pasquils, broached and set on foot, chiefly by the late Usurper, against the blessed memory of our two late soveraigns.' In particular he cites 'The court and character of king James'; and turning to his own target, says :'Let his once mighty lady [i.e. Elizabeth Cromwell] do drudgery to the public.' His chief targets are her alleged thrift and niggardliness, which he regards as unbecoming to the state of high office. After such a tirade, one might expect a fairly remarkable cookery book to follow; but no, it proves to be merely another routine collection.

The Queen's Closet Opened and *The Court and Kitchen of Elizabeth Cromwell,* like all the earlier works with feminine titles, were probably written by men, in an age when authoresses were something of a rarity, just as *The Ladies Cabinet Opened* of 1654 proves to be by Lord Ruthven, and The Countess of Kent's *A Choise Manuall* is another example of the use of a famous name. It is only in the 1680s that the first woman writer who can be positively identified appears – Hannah Wolley; she produced a series of books on domestic management which were very successful and were even translated into German. And a number of private collections of recipes survive, from the late seventeenth century onwards; one example is Anne Blencowe's notebook, which George Saintsbury edited in 1904. This great scholar and authority on wine was puzzled by one recipe, that for *delma*, which turns out to be a very acceptable version of Greek *dolmades*.

Indeed, cookery was becoming cosmopolitan again, as it had been when Arab dishes were introduced to Italy at the beginning of the history of modern western cookery; Turkish, Spanish and Portuguese recipes of varying degrees of authenticity appear in English books. But there was soon to be a reaction against this variety and particularly against the rule of France in English kitchens; French chefs for all their 'musicall-headedness' were still very much in business there, and French recipes were used for everything. The first sign of it came from no less an authority than Patrick Lamb, chef to Queen Anne, in his volume of 1710, in which he extols the advantages of England as a food-producing country and the virtues of English food. Here we may draw our limit, for we are into the world of modern cookery, with its national schools competing rather than supplementing each other. Already many of the late seventeenth-century recipes have a familiar air, and the early eighteenth century saw not only the beginning of English isolationism but the establishment of the groundwork of French *haute cuisine* on which the nineteenth century was to elaborate. Writers like Hannah Glasse have a place in the modern kitchen rather than in the bookcase, and can speak for themselves, even though they antedate the kitchen's industrial revolution in the early nineteenth century, with the introduction of the kitchen range and better control of cooking temperatures. After 1700 there is no need for explanations and interpretations; having come thus far, the reader will have no difficulty in exploring modern cookery without a guide.

English Sixteenth- and Seventeenth-Century Recipes

FLORENTINE OF KIDNEYS
[for 4 persons]

2 pig's kidneys
1 oz breadcrumbs
1 glass sweet sherry
¼ pt cream
pinch nutmeg
marrow of two bones if available

½ lb puff pastry
2 oz ground almonds
1 dsp rosewater
2 eggs
pinch cinnamon

Grill the kidneys until light brown all over (about 5 minutes). Chop coarsely, and mix with all the other ingredients except the pastry. Roll out the pastry into a circle. Place the pastry on an oiled baking tray, so that half the circle is flat on the tray. Place the mixture on this, fold over the other half and seal down with flour and water. Bake at Regulo Mark 4 (370°) for 45 minutes.

Countess of Kent, 1663

CHICKEN WITH GOOSEBERRIES
[for 4 persons]

3 lb chicken
2 pts mutton stock (make with ½ lb
    neck or scrag end if necessary,
    boiling for 1½ hrs)
bouquet garni
½ lb gooseberries
½ oz butter

1 glass dry white wine
½ tsp ground mace
2 oz breadcrumbs
1 tbs dry cider
1 dsp sugar
2 hard-boiled egg yolks

Place the bouquet garni inside the chicken. Boil chicken in stock, adding the wine and the mace, for 75 minutes. Take out the chicken and keep warm on a serving dish. Take off half the stock to cook the gooseberries. Thicken the remaining half with egg yolks and bread-crumbs. Add butter, cider and sugar to other half before cooking gooseberries. Cut up chicken and put in dish with thickened stock and with the drained gooseberries.

Murrell, *Two Bookes of Cookerie*, 1638

FRAGISIE [FRICASSEE] OF CHICKENS [for 4 persons]

3 lb chicken, roasted and carved	*2 eggs*
½ lb artichoke hearts	*lemons*
2 tsp sugar	*2 oz butter*
½ lb cooked gooseberries	*1 tbs dry cider*
1 lettuce	

Wash lettuce and toss lightly in butter over low heat. Beat up eggs, cider and sugar together, and cook chicken meat and gooseberries in this until the eggs are done. Add lettuce and artichoke hearts, garnish with lemons and serve.

Countess of Kent, 1663

LIVERING PUDDINGS [for 2 persons]

¾ lb pig's liver	*2 eggs*
pinch nutmeg	*salt*
pepper	*sausage skin*
2 oz suet	*tbs sultanas*
2 oz breadcrumbs	

Fry liver in oil until lightly brown. Mince finely. Beat eggs whole, and add these and breacdrumbs to liver, together with sultanas and suet. Season. Stuff into sausage skin, and put in saucepan with sufficient water to cover. Bring to the boil and simmer for 20–25 minutes.

Good Houswives Treasurie, c. 1620

DUCK WITH MUSSELS [for 4 persons]

2½ lb duck	*½ tsp cinnamon*
1 qt mussels	*dsp sugar*
pepper	*¼ tsp mace*
½ bottle claret	

Clean mussels and steam until they open. Shell, discarding any suspect ones. Meanwhile roast duck either on spit or in oven. Flour the shelled mussels and fry lightly. Put both these and the roasted duck (cut into pieces) in a casserole, adding the claret, cinnamon, sugar, pepper and mace. Add water to just cover the ingredients and bring to the boil; simmer for 5–10 minutes.

Murrell, *Two Bookes of Cookerie*, 1638

EGGS DRESSED ACCORDING TO THE PORTUGAL MANNER
[for 2 persons]

2 eggs	*4 oz mushrooms*
tsp chopped parsley	*pinch nutmeg*
2 onions	*dsp vinegar*
½ oz breadcrumbs	

Fry parsley and onions in butter. Hardboil eggs and slice into rounds, adding them to the onions. Boil and slice the mushrooms, add them to the previous items and season. Add vinegar when almost cooked, and sprinkle with breadcrumbs and nutmeg to serve.

Marnette, *The Perfect Cook*, 1656

EGGS À LA HUGUENOTE
[for 2 persons]

4 eggs	*pinch grated nutmeg*
juice of ½ lemon	*1 tbs beef stock*
4 oz mushrooms	

Boil mushrooms in ½ inch salted water in a covered pan for 5 minutes. Drain and chop coarsely. Beat all ingredients together in a frying pan over a low flame, adding seasoning. When well mixed and the eggs are cooked, remove and serve with grated nutmeg.

Rabisha, *The Whole Body of Cookery*, 1675

FRENCH PUFFS WITH GREEN HERBS
[for 2 persons]

2 oz spinach	*tbs sugar*
tsp dried savory	*1 lemon*
pinch nutmeg	*2 eggs*
¼ tsp ginger	*½ glass white wine*
tbs chopped parsley	*¼ endive (curly lettuce)*

Chop the spinach and endive finely. Add the parsley and savory and white wine. Season with nutmeg, ginger and sugar and moisten with the eggs to bind. Slice the lemon very thin, and place in frying pan with a little butter. Put one spoonful of the mixture on each slice of lemon, and fry lightly, turning once. Serve with lemon uppermost: this should be squeezed and taken off before eating.

Murrell, *Two Bookes of Cookerie*, 1638

HERRINGS IN ALE [for 4 persons]

3 onions	*1 oz sultanas*
1 lb herring fillets, or 4 herrings	*1 tsp mustard*
¾ pt brown ale	*1 oz breadcrumbs*
pinch saffron	

Cook onions in ale, having chopped them finely, using about half the ale and simmering for 10 minutes. Add the rest of the ale, and the sultanas, mustard and saffron. Put the herrings in a fireproof dish, pour over the ale and onions, and cover. Put in a moderate oven, Regulo Mark 5 (360°) for 30 minutes. Before serving, thicken with breadcrumbs.

A Booke of Cookery, c. 1620

CIMBALS

4 oz flour	*1 pinch aniseed*
1 pinch ground coriander	*3 whites of egg*
4 oz sugar	*1 dsp rosewater*

Sift flour and sugar into a basin. Add coriander and aniseed and mix well. Make a well in the centre, add the egg whites and slowly draw in the flour and sugar. Add the rosewater. Grease two flat baking sheets, and put the paste on it in spoonfuls, to make flat biscuits about 3 inches across. Bake at Regulo Mark 2 (310°) for 30–35 minutes.

Countess of Kent, 1663

HASTIE PUDDING [for 4 persons]

½ pt cream	*1 crushed clove*
½ tsp grated nutmeg	*¼ tsp ground mace*
1 tbs sugar	*1 dsp egg white*
1 egg	*2 oz butter*
¼ tsp ginger	*¼ tsp cinnamon*
3 oz bread in small pieces	*1 tsp flour*

Put cream, bread, nutmeg, clove, mace, cinnamon, ginger and flour in a small saucepan and bring to the boil. Add the butter, beat in the egg and egg white with the sugar. Bring to boil again, and take off heat almost immediately. Turn into a flat dish, put under the grill to brown, and serve sprinkled with sugar.

Rabisha, *Whole Body of Cookery,* 1675

TO MAKE PANCAKES SO CRISPE YOU MAY SET THEM UPRIGHT

Make pancakes according to a conventional recipe, but cook in a

6-inch pan or smaller. When cooked, put a small saucepan containing about ½ lb lard on a low flame, and bring slowly to boil. Drop in pancakes, and boil for 2–3 minutes each.

Murrell, *Two Bookes of Cookerie*, 1638

CAMBRIDGE PUDDING [for 4 persons]

3 oz breadcrumbs	*4 oz suet*
½ tsp grated nutmeg	*1 egg yolk*
2 oz stoned dates	*6 oz flour*
2 eggs	*salt*
1 tbs caster sugar	*⅛ pt milk*
2 oz sultanas	*3 oz butter*
½ tsp cinnamon	

Mix flour, breadcrumbs and suet together. Add milk and eggs and slowly draw in dry ingredients. Add remaining items, except butter, and work until thoroughly mixed. Divide mixture in two. Place half on pudding cloth, and put butter on top. Then place other half of mixture on top and tie cloth firmly at top. Bring 3 pts water to boil, and put pudding in this. Simmer for 45 minutes.

Wolley, *Cook's Guide*, 1664

WHIPT SILLABUB [for 2–4 persons]

½ pt double cream	*2 egg whites*
½ glass sweet sherry or sweet white wine	*1 dsp sugar*

Put one egg white and half the cream into a bowl, and beat until just beginning to become stiff, preferably using birch twigs. Then add remainder of ingredients gradually and beat until thoroughly stiff. Serve, slightly chilled if wished.

Ibid

A RARE CITRON PUDDING [for 2–4 persons]

½ pt single cream	*almonds*
2 eggs	*½ nutmeg, grated*
½ oz candied orange peel	*2 oz candied lemon peel*
2 oz breadcrumbs	*rosewater*
1 oz sugar	

Mix all ingredients and beat thoroughly. Oil a deep basin and flour well. Pour in mixture and tie with a cloth. Bring about 3 pts water to the boil (enough not quite to cover the basin) and boil for 20–25 minutes. Stick with almonds and sprinkle with rosewater before serving.

Elizabeth Cromwell, 1664

The two recipes which follow can be either a sweet savoury or a dessert, though the artichoke pie is really closer to a mince pie than a savoury.

ARTICHOKE PIE [for 4 persons]

6 cooked artichoke hearts
¼ tsp ginger
orange peel (½ orange)
prebaked pastry case
glass sweet sherry
tsp sugar

1 oz raisins
pastry for cover (approx ¾ lb
*   shortcrust in all)*
1 oz butter
2 oz dates
¼ tsp ground mace

Put artichoke hearts, sliced dates, raisins and butter, ginger and mace in case, and cover. Bake at Regulo Mark 3 (320°) for 20 minutes. Boil sweet sherry with sugar and orange peel, remove peel, and add to pie, lifting cover to pour it in. Reseal cover and return to oven for further 20 minutes to finish.

Elizabeth Cromwell, 1664

POTATO PIE [for 4 persons]

1 lb potatoes
¼ tsp cinnamon
pepper
¼ tsp grated nutmeg
¼ lb grapes
¼ lb dates (stoned)

¼ tsp mace
prebaked pastry case
pastry for cover (approx ¾ lb)
¼ pt chicken stock
lemons for garnish
2 oz butter

Boil potatoes in salted water until almost soft. Allow to cool. Season with cinnamon, nutmeg and pepper, chop into cubes. Fill pie, adding dates, mace, peeled and pipped grapes, and butter. Bake at Regulo Mark 3 (320°) for 20 minutes. Take out, lift cover and add chicken stock. Return to oven for 25 minutes to finish.

Marnette, *The Perfect Cook*, 1656

Acknowledgements

p.   7 Homer, *The Iliad*, Penguin, 1949, p. 166.

p. 12 Livy, *Histories*, Dent, Everyman's Library, vol. V, p. 315.

p. 12 Plautus, *Pseudolus*, *Plays*, Loeb Library, Heinemann, 19--, pp. 233, 235.

p. 15 Horace, *Satires*, Loeb Library, Heinemann, 19--, pp. 189, 191.

p. 17 Juvenal, *Satires*, Penguin, 1967, pp. 117-22.

p. 18 Suetonius, *Twelve Caesars*, Penguin, 1957, p. 269.

p. 38 Helen Waddell, *Medieval Latin Lyrics*, Constable, 1948, p. 65.

p. 40 Einhard, *Life of Charlemagne*, Folio Society, 1970, pp. 64, 67.

p. 43 R. Fitzstephen, 'Life of Becket', tr. F. M. Sterton in *Norman Life*, Historical Association, 1934, pp. 34-5.

p. 85 Hartley, *Food in England*, Batsford, 1954, pp. 177-8.

p. 101 J. H. Huizinga, *Waning of the Middle Ages*, New York, Doubleday, 1954, pp. 252-3.

p. 110 Coryat, *Crudities*, Maclehose, 1905, vol. I, p. 236.

Index

Index